Sefer Pesukei Torah

Passages of Torah

Written by
Reb Moshe
Steinerman

Edited by Elise Teitelbaum

Reb Moshe Steinerman

iloveTorah Jewish Outreach Network

iloveTorah Jewish Publishing
First Published 2018
ISBN: 978-1-947706-02-6

Editor: Elise Teitelbaum
Co Editor: Rochel Steinerman

Artwork by Boris Shapiro
Book Format by Rabbi Benyamin
Fleischman

ABOUT THE AUTHOR

Rabbi Moshe Steinerman grew up as a religious Jew on the hillsides of Maryland. During his teenage years, Reb Moshe developed his talent for photography, while connecting to nature and speaking to *HaShem*. He later found his path through Breslov *Chassidus*, while maintaining closeness to the *Litvish* style of learning. He studied in the Baltimore yeshiva, Ner Yisrael; then married and moved to Lakewood, New Jersey. After settling down, he began to write *Kavanos Halev*, with the blessing of Rav Malkiel Kotler *Shlita*, Rosh Yeshiva of Beis Medrash Gevoha.

After establishing one of the first Jewish outreach websites, ilovetorah.com in 1996, Reb Moshe's teachings became popular among the full spectrum of Jews, from the unaffiliated to ultra-Orthodox. His teachings, including hundreds of stories of tzaddikim, gained popularity due to the ideal of drawing Jews together. Reb Moshe made aliyah to Tzfat in 2003 than later moved with his wife and children, to Jerusalem, in 2012. He has been helping to return English-speaking Jews to Judaism through his numerous Jewish videos and audio shiurim. His learning experience includes the completion of both Talmud Bavli and Yerushalmi as well as other important works.

Some of his other books are Kavanos Halev (Meditations of Heart), Tikkun Shechinah, Tovim Meoros (Glimpse of Light), Chassidus, Kabbalah & Meditation, Yom Leyom (Day by Day), Pathways of the Righteous, Prayers of the Heart, A Journey into Holiness, and The True Intentions of the Baal Shem Tov.

Special thanks to Rabbi Benyamin Fleischman for making the books into print-ready format and to Elise Teitelbaum for helping to edit the books.

Dedications

*In Memory of my father, Reb Shlomo Zavel
Ben Yaakov zt"l, and my father-in-law Reb
Menachem ben Reuven zt"l.
My grandparents Yaakov Ben Zavel, Toba
Esther bas Gedlaya Aharon Hakohein, Yehudah
ben Ike, Isabbela Bas Israel
My great-grandmother Nechama bas Sara
Rivka, My Uncle Shmuel Yosef ben Gedalya
Aharon Hakohein
May they all have an aliyah in shamayim.*

I grew up in a house filled with the *Torah* learning of my father, who studied most of the day. Although there were no Jews in this remote part of Maryland, my father was a man of *chesed* to all people and was known for his brilliance in *Torah* scholarship.

I want to say a special thank you to the Nikolsburg Rebbe and the Biala Rebbe for their encouragement and blessings. Most of all, I offer thanks to my wife, Rochel, for her faithful support.

Someone once asked me why I write Torah books. I explained that I write Torah in order to leave a legacy for my children and grandchildren. So that they should understand how to serve Hashem. I wish my father left me with more than just memories of his learning Torah and avodas Hashem. I wish he left me a book, a blueprint of his soul, so that I could remember all the divrey Torah he spoke to me.

Dear Reader,

Ilovetorah Jewish Outreach is a non-profit organization; books and Torah classes are available at low cost. Therefore, we appreciate your donation to help Rabbi Moshe Steinerman and ilovetorah.com to continue their work on behalf of the Jewish people. We also ask that you pass on these books to others once you are finished with them.

Thank you,
Reb Moshe Steinerman
www.ilovetorah.com
Donations:
www.ilovetorah.com/donations

RABBINIC APPROVALS / HASKAMAHS

בס"ד

RABBI DOVID B. KAPLAN
RABBI OF WEST NEW YORK
5308 PALISADE AVENUE • WEST NEW YORK, NJ 07093
201-867-6859 • WESTNEWYORKSHUL@GMAIL.COM

דוד ברוך הלוי קאפלאן
רב ואב"ד דק"ק
וועסט ניו יארק

י' שבט ה'תשע"ז / February 6, 2017

Dear Friends,

Shalom and Blessings!

For approximately twenty years I have followed the works of Rabbi Moshe Steinerman, Shlit"a, a pioneer in the use of social media to encourage people and bring them closer to G-d.

Over the years Rabbi Steinerman has produced, and made public at no charge, hundreds of videos sharing his Torah wisdom, his holy stories, and his touching songs. Rabbi Steinerman has written a number of books, all promoting true Jewish Torah spirituality. Rabbi Steinerman's works have touched many thousands of Jews, and even spirituality-seeking non-Jews, from all walks of life and at all points of the globe.

Rabbi Steinerman is a tomim (pure-hearted one) in the most flattering sense of the word.

I give my full approbation and recommendation to all of Rabbi Steinerman's works.

I wish Rabbi Steinerman much success in all his endeavors.

May G-d bless Rabbi Moshe Steinerman, his wife, Rebbetzin Rochel Steinerman, and their beautiful children; and may G-d grant them health, success, and nachas!

With blessings,

Rabbi Dovid B. Kaplan

Approval of the Biala Rebbe of New York/Miami/Betar

הובא לפני גליונות בעניני קירוב רחוקים לקרב אחינו בני ישראל אל
אביהם שבשמים, כידוע מהבעש"ט זיע"א שאמר "אימתי קאתי מר
לכשיפוצו מעינותיך חוצה" ואפריון נמטי"ה להאי גברא יקירא מיקירי
צפת עיה"ק תובב"א כמע"כ מוהר"ר משה שטיינרמן שליט"א אשר כבר
עוסק רבות בשנים לקרב רחוקים לתורה וליהדות, וכעת מוציא לאור
ספר כשם "פסוקי תורה" וראיתי דברים נחמדים מאוד וניכר מתוך
הדברים שהרב בעל המחבר - אהבת השי"ת ואהבת התורה וישראל
בלבבו, ובטחוני כי הספר יביא תועלת גדולה לכל עם ישראל.

ויה"ר שיזכה לבוא לגומרה ברוב פאר והדר ונזכה לגאולתן של ישראל
בב"א.

בכבוד רב:
אהרן שלמה חיים אליעזר
בלאאו"ר שלמה ה אבי"שלא

Reb Moshe Steinerman

Rabbi M. Lebovits
Grand Rabbi of
Nikolsburg
53 Decatur Avenue
Spring Valley, N.Y. 10977

יוסף יחיאל מיכל
לעבאוויטש
ניקלשבורג
מאנסי - ספרינג וואלי, נ. י.

בעזהשי"ת

בשורותי אלו באתי להעיד על מעשה אומן, מופלא מופלג בהפלגת חכמים ונבונים,
ירא וחרד לדבר ה', ומשתוקק לקרב לבית ישראל לאביהם שבשמים,
ה"ה הרב **משה שטיינערמאן** שליט"א בעיה"ק צפת תובב"א

שעלה בידו להעלות על הספר דברים נפלאים שאסף מספרים הקדושים, בענין אהבה
אהוה שלום ורעיות. לראות מעלות חברינו ולא חסרונם, עי"ז להיות נמנעים מדברי
ריבות ומחלוקת. ולתקן עון שנאת חנם אשר בשכיל זה נחרב בית מקדשינו
ותפארתינו, וכמשאחז"ל (ירושלמי ובבלי יומא ט ע"ב) על ויהן שם ישראל, שניתנה תורה באופן
שהנו שם כאיש אחד בלב אחד.

וניכר בספר כי עמל ויגע הרבה להוציא מתח"י דבר נאה ומתוקן, ע"כ אף ידי תכון
עמו להוציא לאור עולם, ויהי רצון שחפץ ה' בידו יצליח, ויברך ה' חילו ופועל ידו
תרצה. שיברך על המוגמר להגדיל תורה ולהאדירה ולהפיצו בקרב ישראל, עד ביאת
גוא"צ בב"א.

א"ד הכותב לכבוד התורה ומרביציה,
י"ט חשון תשמ"י

[signature]

Rabbi Abraham Y. S. Friedman
161 Maple Avenue #C Spring Valley NY 10977
Tel: 845-425-5043 Fax: 845-425-8045

רב דביהמ"ד אמרי"י שפ"ר קאמאדא
ראש כולל יאר"י

בעזהשי"ת

ישפות השם החיים והשלו', לכבוד ידידי מאז ומקדם מיקירי קרתא
דירושלים יראה שלם, זוכה ומזכה אחרים, להיות דבוק באלקינו, ה"ה
הר"ר משה שטיינרמאן שליט"א.

שמחתי מאוד לשמוע ממך, מאתר רחוק וקירוב הלבבות, בעסק
תורתך הקדושה ועבודתך בלי לאות, וכה יעזור ה' להלאה ביתר שאת
ויתר עז. והנה שלחת את הספר שלקטת בעניני דביקות בה', לקרב
לבבות בני ישראל לאבינו שבשמים בשפת אנגלית, אבל דא עקא
השפה לא ידענו, ע"כ לא זכיתי לקרותו, ע"א א"א לי ליתן הסכמה פרטי
על ספרך. ובכלל קיבלתי על עצמי שלא ליתן הסכמות, ובפרט כשאין
לי פנאי לקרות הספר מתחלתו עד סופו, אבל בכלליות זכרתי לך חסד
נעוריך. היאך הי' המתיקות שלך בעבדות השם פה בעירינו, ובנועם
המדות, וחזקה על חבר שאינו מוציא מתחת ידו דבר שאינו מותקן,
ובפרט שכל מגמתך להרבות כבוד שמים, שבודאי סייעתא דשמיא
ילוה כל ימיך לראות רב נחת מיוצ"ח ומפרי ידיך, שתתקבל הספר
בסבר פנים יפות אצל אחינו בני ישראל שמדברים בשפת האנגלית
שיתקרבו לאבינו שבשמים ולהדבק בו באמת לאות נפשך, ולהרבות
פעלים לתורה ועבודה וקדושה בדביקות עם מדות טובות, בנייחותא
נייחא בעליונים ונייחא בתחתונים עד ביאת גואל צדק בב"א.

כ"ד ידידך השמח בהצלחתך ובעבודתך

אברהם יחזקאל שרגא פרידמאן

Reb Moshe Steinerman

Introduction

Every passage of Torah can be interpreted in a simple interpretation, or it can be uncovered to show many secret meanings. Reb Moshe tries to show the reader practical advice through both methods of uncovering. Using the many forms of *gematria*, he tries to connect ideas between passages and words from Tanach. He shows a much deeper connection one can find when studying the texts with an open mind, allowing the passages to open and the words to flow in a new light.

These new Torah thoughts, called *chiddushim*, are based on a vast knowledge of Tanach and Talmud, even weaving Kabbalistic teachings into the *pesukim*. While doing so, his main purpose is still to keep the book very practical and to bear fruitful advice to his followers.

The beauty behind *gematrias* is sometimes overlooked and not appreciated for its greatness. The Baal Shem Tov taught: "When *Mashiach* comes (may it be speedily in our days) he will explain the entire Torah from beginning to end, according to all the letter combinations within each word. Then he will combine the entire Torah into one word, which will contain letter combinations beyond calculations. [Moshiach] will explain them all, as well." (T'shuos Chein, Tazria)

Since Reb Moshe uses many *gematria* types in this book, it is good to gain a basic understanding of them.

There are many different methods to decipher the hidden *gematrias* and secrets of words. Here are some of them:

❖ מספר הכרחי Mispar Hechrachi (Mispar ha-Panim, absolute, standard, normative value) is the most commonly used method of calculating gematria where each of the 22 letters is assigned a basic value.

ת	ש	ר	ק	צ	פ	ע	ס	נ	מ	ל	כ	י	ט	ח	ז	ו	ה	ד	ג	ב	א
400	300	200	100	90	80	70	60	50	40	30	20	10	9	8	7	6	5	4	3	2	1

❖ מספר גדול *Mispar Gadol* (**large value**) is similar to the standard method, but final (*sofit*) letters are counted as a continuation of the alphabet and are valued from 500 to 900 instead of being included as the regular letter.

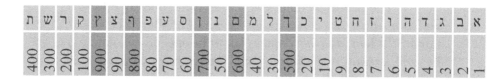

❖ מספר סידורי *Mispar Siduri* (**ordinal value**) assigns each letter a number ranging from 1 to 22 in the order of the alphabet.

ת	ש	ר	ק	צ	פ	ע	ס	נ	מ	ל	כ	י	ט	ח	ז	ו	ה	ד	ג	ב	א
22	21	20	19	18	17	16	15	14	13	12	11	10	9	8	7	6	5	4	3	2	1

❖ מספר קטן *Mispar Katan (Mispar Meugal*, **reduced value**) is the value of the letters but without the zeros after large numbers. (ex. "*Lamed*" is 3 instead of 30, "Shin" is 3 instead of 300).

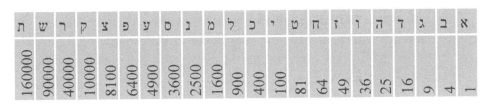

ת	ש	ר	ק	צ	פ	ע	ס	נ	מ	ל	כ	י	ט	ח	ז	ו	ה	ד	ג	ב	א
4	3	2	1	9	8	7	6	5	4	3	2	1	9	8	7	6	5	4	3	2	1

❖ **מספר הפרטי** *Mispar Perati (Mispar HaMerubah HaPerati)* assigns each letter its standard value as a squared number. (ex. "*Aleph*" = 1 x 1 = 1, "*Gimel*" = 3 x 3 = 9).

ת	ש	ר	ק	צ	פ	ע	ס	נ	מ	ל	כ	י	ט	ח	ז	ו	ה	ד	ג	ב	א
160000	90000	40000	10000	8100	6400	4900	3600	2500	1600	900	400	100	81	64	49	36	25	16	9	4	1

❖ **מספר שמי\מילוי** *Mispar Shemi (Milui*, **full name value)** values each letter as the value of the letter's name. (ex. "*Aleph*" = 1 + 30 + 80 = 111). However, there is more than one way to spell each letter.

ת	ש	ר	ק	צ	פ	ע	ס	נ	מ	ל	כ	י	ט	ח	ז	ו	ה	ד	ג	ב	א
406	360	510	186	104	81	130	120	106	80	74	100	20	419	418	77	22	6	434	73	412	111

❖ **מספר מוספי** *Mispar Musafi* adds the number of letters in the word or phrase to the value.

❖ **אתב״ש** *AtBash* exchanges each letter's value for its opposite letter's value. (ex. "*Aleph*" switches values with "*Tav*", "*Daled*" switches values with "*Kuf*").

כ	י	ט	ח	ז	ו	ה	ד	ג	ב	א
ל	מ	נ	ס	ע	פ	צ	ק	ר	ש	ת

❖ **אלב"ם** *AlBam* splits the alphabet in half and letters from the first half switch values with letters from the second half. (ex. *"Aleph"* switches values with *"Lamed"*, *"Vav"* switches values with *"Pey"*).

כ	י	ט	ח	ז	ו	ה	ד	ג	ב	א
ת	ש	ר	ק	צ	פ	ע	ס	נ	מ	ל

❖ **מספר בונה** *Mispar Bone'eh* (building value) does exactly as the name describes. It adds the value of all previous letters in the word to the value of the current letter as the word is calculated. (ex. *Echad* is $1 + (1 + 8) + (1 + 8 + 4) = 23$).

❖ **מספר קדמי** *Mispar Kidmi* (also called *Mispar Meshulash*, **triangular value**) adds the value of all preceding letters in the alphabet to each letter's value. (ex. *"Aleph"* = 1, *"Beis"* = 1 + 2 = 3, *"Gimmel"* = 1 + 2 + 3 = 6).

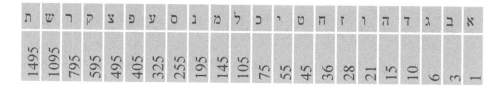

ת	ש	ר	ק	צ	פ	ע	ס	נ	מ	ל	כ	י	ט	ח	ז	ו	ה	ד	ג	ב	א
1495	1095	795	595	495	405	325	255	195	145	105	75	55	45	36	28	21	15	10	6	3	1

❖ **מספר נעלם** *Mispar Ne'elam* (hidden value) values each letter as the value of the letter's name excluding the letter itself. (ex. *"Aleph"* = 30 + 80 = 110).

ת	ש	ר	ק	צ	פ	ע	ס	נ	מ	ל	כ	י	ט	ח	ז	ו	ה	ד	ג	ב	א
6	60	310	86	14	—	60	60	56	40	44	80	10	410	410	70	16	—	430	70	410	110

❖ מספר המרובע הכללי *Mispar HaMerubah HaKlali* is the standard value squared.

❖ מספר משולש *Mispar Meshulash* (cubed value, triangular value) values each letter as its value cubed. (ex. "*Aleph*" = 1 x 1 x 1 = 1, "*Beis*" = 2 x 2 x 2 = 8).

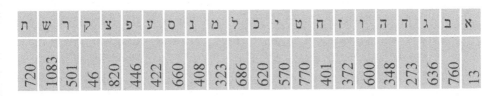

ת	ש	ר	ק	צ	פ	ע	ס	נ	מ	ל	כ	י	ט	ח	ז	ו	ה	ד	ג	ב	א
64000000	27000000	8000000	1000000	729000	512000	343000	216000	125000	64000	27000	8000	1000	729	512	343	216	125	64	27	8	1

❖ מספר האחור *Mispar Ha'achor* (sometimes called *Mispar Meshulash*, triangular value) values each letter as its value multiplied by the position of the letter in the word or phrase.

❖ מספר מספרי *Mispar Mispari* spells out the Hebrew name of each of the letter's standard values and adds up their values. (ex. "*Aleph*" = one (*Echad*) = 1 + 8 + 4 = 13).

ת	ש	ר	ק	צ	פ	ע	ס	נ	מ	ל	כ	י	ט	ח	ז	ו	ה	ד	ג	ב	א
720	1083	501	46	820	446	422	660	408	323	686	620	570	770	401	372	600	348	273	636	760	13

❖ מספר קטן מספרי *Mispar Katan Mispari* (integral reduced value) is the digital root of the standard value. This is obtained by adding all the digits in the number until the number is a single digit. (ex. *Echad* (13) --> 1 + 3 --> 4).

❖ מספר כלל *Mispar Kolel* is the value plus adding the number of words in the phrase.

❖ אכב"י *AchBi* splits the alphabet in half and within each group, the first letter switches with the last letter and the second with the tenth, etc. (ex. *"Aleph"* switches with *"Chaf"*, *"Hey"* switches with *"Zayin"*, *"Mem"*switches *"Shin"*).

פ	ע	ס	נ	מ	ל		ו	ה	ד	ג	ב	א
	צ	ק	ר	ש	ת		ז	ח	ט	י	כ	

❖ **אטב״ח** *AtBach* splits the alphabet into three groups of nine including the final (*sofit*) letters at the end. Within each group, the first letter switches with the last letter and the second with the eighth, etc. (ex. *"Aleph"* switches with *"Tes"*, *"Lamid"* switches with *"Ayin"*, *"Yud"* switches *"Tzadi"*, *"Kuf"* switches *"Final Tzadi"*).

ך	ת	ש	ר	ק		נ	מ	ל	כ	י		ה	ד	ג	ב	א
	ם	ן	ף	ץ		ס	ע	פ	צ			ו	ז	ח	ט	

❖ **אי״ק בכ״ר** *Ayak Bachar* (or *Ayak Bakar*) splits the alphabet into three groups of nine including the final (*sofit*) letters at the end. The letters in the first group replace the ones in the second group, the letters in the second group replace the ones in the third group, and the letters in the third group replace the ones in the first group. (ex. *"Aleph"* takes the place of *"Yud"*, *"Yud"* takes the place of *"Kuf"*, *"Kuf"* takes the place of *"Aleph"*, *"Beis"* takes the place of *"Chaf"* etc.).

ט	ח	ז	ו	ה	ד	ג	ב	א
צ	פ	ע	ס	נ	מ	ל	כ	י
ץ	ף	ז	ם	ד	ת	ש	ר	ק

❖ **אופנים** *Ofanim* replaces each letter with the last letter of its name. (ex. *"Aleph"* becomes *"Fey"*, *"Lamid"* becomes *"Daled"*).

א	ב	ג	ד	ה	ו	ז	ח	ט	י	כ	ל	מ	נ	ס	ע	פ	צ	ק	ר	ש	ת
ת	ל	ת	א	ו	ד	ד	מ	ד	פ	ד	ת	ת	ו	ו	א	י	פ	ש	ו	ו	ף

❖ **אח״ס בט״ע** *Achas Beta* splits the alphabet into groups of 7, 7, and 8 letters. The letters in the first group exchange the ones in the second group, the letters in the second group swap the ones in the third group, and the letters in the third group replace the ones in the first group. The letter *"Tav"* does not change.

❖ **אבג״ד** *Avgad* trades each letter with the next one. (ex. *"Aleph"* becomes *"Beis"*, *"Beis"* becomes *"Gimmel"*, *"Tav"* becomes *"Aleph"*).

א	ב	ג	ד	ה	ו	ז	ח	ט	י	כ	ל	מ	נ	ס	ע	פ	צ	ק	ר	ש	ת
ב	ג	ד	ה	ו	ז	ח	ט	י	כ	ל	מ	נ	ס	ע	פ	צ	ק	ר	ש	ת	א

❖ **Reverse** *Avgad* swaps each letter with the previous one. (ex. *"Beis"* becomes *"Aleph"*, *"Gimmel"* becomes "Beis", *"Aleph"* becomes *"Tav"*).

א	ב	ג	ד	ה	ו	ז	ח	ט	י	כ	ל	מ	נ	ס	ע	פ	צ	ק	ר	ש	ת
ת	א	ב	ג	ד	ה	ו	ז	ח	ט	י	כ	ל	מ	נ	ס	ע	פ	צ	ק	ר	ש

Reb Moshe Steinerman

Table of Contents

Lesson 1

"לַי-ה-וָ-ה הַיְשׁוּעָה; עַל-עַמְּךָ בִרְכָתֶךָ
סֶּלָה"

"Salvation belongs to the L-rd; Your blessing be upon Your people, Selah." (Psalms 3:9)

Life has its ups and downs that are there to strengthen us in our service of *Hashem*. Even though we are taught to, "Call to *Hashem*, and He will answer", we must still do the calling. Calling alone isn't enough though; we must, "lift up our eyes on high, and see who created these?" (Isaiah 40:26). This is because "Salvation belongs to *Hashem*." (Psalms 3:9).

Many of us make a mistake thinking that salvation is in our own hands or in the hands of mankind. "Some rely on chariots and some on horses..." (Psalms 20:8). It is easy to pretend and talk about belief in *Hashem* but to live and breathe it is a different world. The *posuk* continues, "but as for us, on the name of *Hashem*, our G-d, we call." (ibid) Why does the *posuk* say "on the Name of *Hashem*"? To call something by name, you must know something about it. When you're at a point in life when you can call on *Hashem's* Name, and understand that He is your only salvation, that is when He is "our [your] G-d" (ibid). Then, Your blessing be upon Your people *Selah* (Psalms 3:9). Blessing, therefore, comes when a person knows *Hashem's* Name and believes only in His salvation.

The *posuk* says, "And G-d called the light day, and the darkness He called night." (Genesis 1:5) The word for 'לאור, the light' has a *gematria* of 237. If you take the first letter of each word of the *posuk*, "salvation belongs to the L-rd; Your blessing be upon Your people *Selah*" (Psalms 3:9), להעעבס you also have the *gematria* 237 because when a person believes with perfect faith in *Hashem's* salvation, his entire life is filled with

23

light and blessing flows down from on high to all the worlds.
When you add the *gematria* for each of the last letters of the
posuk, ההלדדה you come to the value of 85. If you add this to
237, you find the word *viyemasru* (value of 322) 'and were
delivered', as in the *posuk*, "So they were delivered, out of the
thousands of Israel, a thousand of every tribe, twelve thousand
armed for war." (Numbers 31:5)

The idea of a thousand has significance in the idea of
salvation and redemption. It also says in the book of Numbers
31:4, "Of every tribe a thousand, throughout all the tribes of
Israel, shall you send to war."

If you take the passage, "Salvation belongs to the L-rd;
Your blessing be upon Your people *Selah*." (Psalms 3:9), and
you add the numerical value of each word in the gematria style
of Reverse *Avgad*, you get a total of 999.

ל-יְ-הֹ-וָ-ה = 42
הַיְשׁוּעָה = 282
עַל = 80
עַמְּךָ = 100
בִרְכָתֶךָ = 421
סֶּלָה = 74

If you then add one for the entire *posuk*, you get a total
of 1000. "He remembered His covenant forever, the word
which He commanded to a thousand generations." (Psalms
105:8)

"He has remembered your covenant forever, the word
which He commanded to a thousand generations which He
made with Avraham, and his oath to Yitzchak; and confirmed
the same to Yacov for a law, and to Israel for an everlasting
covenant." (Psalms 105:8)

"A thousand years are like one day. For a thousand
years are in Your eyes like yesterday which passed, and a watch
in the night." (Psalms 84:11)

If you take the word אלף *Elef*, which means a thousand,
you also spell out the first Hebrew letter which is *Alef*. Alef
also represents the oneness of *Hashem*. There is one *Hashem*

and no other; when you believe this wholeheartedly, your life is filled with salvation and blessing.

Elef which is *Alef* has the numeric value of 111 which also shares the word, 'להמול LiHeMol', to be circumcised. Like it said in the *posuk* mentioned above in the Psalms, "He has remembered your covenant forever." (Psalms 105:8) When a person's heart is circumcised, completely devoted to *Hashem*, He remembers the guarantee as the *posuk* continues, "Which He made as a treaty with Abraham and which was His oath to Issac, and He established it for Jacob as a statute, for Israel as an everlasting covenant." (Psalms 105:9-10) *Hashem* will, therefore, protect those who accept Him as one, like the *Alef* which is equivalent to one.

Also sharing the numeric value of 111 (להמול *LiHeMol*, be circumcised) is the 'עולה *(karbon) olah*,' the burnt offerings sent up to *Hashem* in the times of the *Bais Hamikdash*. So, when you circumcise your heart when you serve *Hashem* with complete devotion, then you will see miracles in your life. Reverse the word *Elef* and *Alef*, and you have the word פלא *Peleh*, wonder, meaning miracle.

So, what is a miracle? It is separated and independent from the laws of the physical world. It is also influenced by hidden forces that link the mystical and transcendental planes. In Sefer Yetzirah (2:3 p.11), it explains that the first letter, *Peh*, is pronounced with the lips, the second letter, *Lamed*, with the middle of the tongue, and the final *Alef* with the throat. Thus, the first letter is pronounced with the outermost revealed part of the mouth, while the last is voiced with the innermost concealed part. The word פלא *Peleh* thus denotes the transition from the revealed to the concealed.

You can note that if you multiply 111, 1x1x1, you return to the number of 1. Therefore, if you see wonders in your life, you must attribute them back to their source, *Hashem*. He is constantly showering upon us salvation at every moment and in all affairs of our life. You cannot just pass them off as chance, but you must break them down very often and show thanks to the One who is watching over you and taking care of your every need. Therefore, salvation truly does come from *Hashem*, when we put Him first in our life.

"I lift my head to the mountains: from where my help will come?" (Psalms 121:1) Why does Dovid Hamelech start this Psalm with a question? It is because he understands that every day we will be tried and tested to see if we truly believe in *Hashem*. Every day is filled with its own unique challenges and new experiences that can lead us closer towards *Hashem* or astray if we should choose to give up. "I lift my head to the mountains," because literally, this new day feels as if a mountain is being held over my head, ready to squash the hard work I performed yesterday in order to come close to You (*Hashem*).

We are told that every day we should accept the Torah like it was given to us anew, similar to our experience on *Har Sinai*. What was our experience there?

"ויתיצבו בתחתית ההר"

"They stood at the foot of [lit. under] the mountain." (Exodus 19:17).

The Gemara (Shabbos 88a) says that by stating *"betachtis hahar"* - lit. "in the bottom of the mountain"- the *posuk* teaches that *Hashem* lifted the mountain and covered the people with it as though it were a large, overturned barrel.

When *Hashem* offered the Jewish people the Torah, they immediately responded *"Na'aseh venishma"*- "We will do, and we will listen (study)." If so, why was it necessary for Him to suspend the mountain over them and warn them that if they did not accept the Torah they would be killed (see Gemara, Shabbos 88a)?

Hashem was warning us: every day you're going to feel as if there is a mountain wishing to obliterate you; only if you accept me as your savior will you persevere through this new day. Dovid Hamelech is reminding us that every day we are going to question why life feels like a huge mountain that must be climbed anew, all the way from the bottom again. It is okay to start over and feel this burden because we just should

26

remember, "My help comes from *Hashem*, Maker of heaven and earth. He will not let your foot slip, He will not slumber - Your Guardian." (Psalms 121:2-3)

What should we expect from *Hashem's* salvation? Are our hopes to be the same as *Hashem's*? If our salvation is not exactly as we expect it to be, we feel angry and disappointed in *Hashem*. If our expectations are not realistic, why should we bother having them? They only end up making us feel downtrodden and confused.

When *Hashem* wants to give us blessing, He sees the vessel that we have, and He fills it up appropriately. If the blessing would overflow, it could damage the vessel. Should *Hashem* give it over too hot or too cold, the vessel could also break. *Hashem's* blessing must be calculated, based on what we can handle and what is truly best for us. However, when we see ourselves with tainted eyes, not seeing the full picture, we imagine salvation as different from what is realistic or even good for us. In the book of Deuteronomy (11:15) it says, "And I will give grass in your fields for your cattle and you will eat and you will be satisfied." How can *Hashem* imply satisfaction when I am not happy? I didn't get exactly what I had wanted.

"יוֹרֶה וּמַלְקוֹשׁ"   *"Yoreh oomalkosh"*

"That I will give rain to your land, the early and the late rains, that you may gather in your grain, your wine, and your oil." (Deuteronomy 11:14) Timing is everything in life. If the same rainfall or blessing in your life arrives earlier or later than needed, it could have a worsening effect instead of a blessing. On *Rosh Hashanah*, we are judged not only for how many blessings we will receive that year, but also when it should arrive. Why? Because timing is everything. *Chazal* asks, what happens to the person who didn't repent for the new year, but two months down the road becomes a righteous person? While *Hashem* doesn't change the amount of blessing, which must be decided on *Rosh Hashanah*, He adjusts the timing of his sustenance that it should arrive at a more appropriate time to help him. The opposite is also true; the person who repents for the new year and then turns around and becomes more sinful, his original allotment for the new year comes at a less opportune time. Now let us return to the original *posuk*, "salvation belongs to the L-rd; Your blessing be upon Your people *Selah*." (Psalms 3:9) It is the word *Selah* that is a seal from *Hashem*, that He will forever take care of our needs. The word סֶלָה *Selah* (95) has the numeric value of המן *HaMan*, the *man* which was given to the people to sustain them. The *man* is symbolic of our receiving what we need from *Hashem* in the way that we deserve. To those who were righteous, their *man* arrived on their doorstep already prepared. For those lacking in holiness and faith, they had to go out to receive their portion and then prepare it themselves.

As you can see, everything in our life is calculated and weighed by our deeds. We cannot hide under the radar but we must eventually confront our misdeeds, take them by the reins, and fix up our lives to serve *Hashem* in truth since life is short. Because הימים *HaYomim*, the days' (95) of our years in them [total] seventy years, and with strength, eighty years (Psalms 90:10).

Hashem's promise to us of a covenant and protection forever isn't enough; it takes our appreciation of life, the value of each day, to live a life that is full. What is a full life? Rava, from the house of Eli, studied Torah and lived to the age of forty. Abayey was also from the house of Eli; he also studied Torah, but he lived till sixty years of age. Why the difference? Explains the Talmud: because he also performed kindness to others (Rosh Hashanah 18). Now we can't imagine that Rava didn't do kind acts in his life. He was obviously a great scholar with tremendous *midos*, but Abayey lived for helping others. He enthroned his entire life around both the study of Torah and helping others. It isn't just the years of a person's life that are important, but rather it is how he spends it. If years were so important why was Adam, the first man, willing to forego seventy years of his life to Dovid Hamelech?

The Gemarah explains that *Hashem* showed Adam the history of mankind - each generation and its leaders. (Avoda

Zara 5a) During this exhibition, Adam was shown the soul of Dovid Hamelech and saw that he was destined to live only a short time. Grieved at the loss of potential, he inquired whether it was possible to bequeath some of his own years to Dovid Hamelech. *Hashem* answered that Adam was destined to live for 1000 years (*Elef*), but he would be allowed to give up some of those years to Dovid Hamelech. Adam then bequeathed seventy years to Dovid, so that Adam lived for 930 years instead of 1000.

Chazal explain that when the last year of Adam's life arrived, he regretted what he had done and wanted to take it back but eventually agreed to keep his promise. Rav Chaim Zaitchik interprets that Adam HaRishon (as with all *tzaddikim*) cherished life so much that, as he was approaching death, he could not bear to forgo the opportunity he had to accomplish more with those extra years. There is so much that a sage can do with even one more year, with even one more month, with even a single day. Life is so precious that when he realized his time was up, he became so distraught and irrational that he forgot his promise or was willing to retract the promise.

When a person is young and hasn't attained his full wisdom, he doesn't have a full perspective on life. It was during Adam's younger years that he was simply willing to give up his own lifespan. However, when he became older and wiser, he started to realize how much he could accomplish with even one more day of his own, let alone one more year. As the parent for future generations, he had to reflect on what was truly important, his descendants, that they have a leader in the future.

The *gematria* for אדם Adam is forty-five, as well as the word הוליד *HoLeid*, which means to have offspring. Even though Adam gave up his 'time' so to speak to the future leader of Israel, he really gave up nothing; it was as if he fathered him. The merits of a father and mother continue with the *mitzvos* of their offspring. My wife always reminds me, it's not babysitting when you're watching your own children; it's a *mitzvah*. Stop complaining and be happy to care for the next generation. We are living now for them; their Torah is our Torah.

"Salvation belongs to the L-rd; Your blessing be upon Your people *Selah*" (Psalms 3:9). How do we become this blessed nation that *Hashem* speaks about in the *posuk*? If you take the word עַמְּךָ *amcha*, Your people, and you change the *nikudos*, vowel points, you have the word *emach*, with you. When we are *Hashem's* people, when we are personally with *Hashem*, that is when we will see the salvation and blessing that belongs to *Hashem*. Then the covenant of our forefathers protects us and showers us from on High.

Lesson 2

"כִּי שֶׁבַע יִפּוֹל צַדִּיק וָקָם וּרְשָׁעִים
יִכָּשְׁלוּ בְרָעָה"

"A righteous man falls down seven times and gets up." — Shlomo Hamelech (Proverbs, 24:16)

This leaves us the question of what does the righteous man do? He never gives up and never throws in the towel. Rather he sees his downfall as an opportunity to start anew.

If you take the first letters of every word of the *posuk* and calculate them, you receive the numerical value of 444. Sharing this total is the word, ילדת *Yoledes*, bear. The idea of bearing and becoming new is the idea of seven. There are seven-thousand years of the world; there are seven days of the week which *Hashem* gave birth to and seventy years of the Jubilee cycle.

If you take the last letters of every word ה-יעלקממו and calculate them, you obtain the numerical value of 301. This is also the word, שא *sa* (301), which means to lift up and forgive. "Forgive the trespass of the servants of *Hashem* of your father." (Genesis 50:17) In order to lift ourselves back up, we need forgiveness from Heaven. What is remarkable about forgiveness is how *Hashem* many times has already forgiven us before we even confess our sins. "[When] I said, 'I will confess my transgressions to *Hashem*', You had [already] forgiven the iniquity of my sin, *Selah*." (Psalms 32:5)

Sharing the value of 301 is also the word רפאך *Rofecha* (301) that heals you. After one falls, he is healed both physically and spiritually. It is this fall that heals you and that returns your soul with new excitement to serve *Hashem*. Like the word אש *esh*, fire (301), it rekindles your soul and enables you to serve *Hashem* all anew.

Daniel and his friends were put to the test of fire being heated seven times more than normal to show that a righteous man is tested seven times and can leave unscathed from anything blocking his path. Nebuchadnezzar was hoping the four scholars had a limit to their faith in *Hashem* and under enough torture would conspire against *Hashem*. Tossing the *rabbis* into the flames and seeing no results, "Nebuchadnezzar was filled with fury... He exclaimed and commanded [his men] to heat the furnace seven times more than it was normally heated..." He explained and said, "Behold, I see four unbound men walking in the fire, and there is no wound on them; and the appearance of the fourth [one] is like an angel's." (Daniel 3:19-26)

In life, we are constantly tested to see if we remain faithful to *Hashem*. It may not be through actual fire but, in our own way, we each get thrown into the confusions of the world, with the ultimate goal of leaving unfazed.

Let us now return to the *posuk*, "[When] I said, 'I will confess my transgressions to *Hashem*', You had [already] forgiven the iniquity of my sin, *Selah.*" (Psalms 32:5) Why would *Hashem* already forgive someone before he confesses to Him? Doesn't that defeat the logic of repentance? Well, there are many types of sins. There are sins that a person does accidentally and those he actually runs after purposely. One's accidental sins are greater in number than those done purposefully. I mean, who in his right mind would sin against *Hashem* while at that very moment He is shedding light, giving him the very breath which he uses against Him? (Tomer Devorah 1) Maybe then you could say that almost all sins are because a person loses his mind in some way.

"*Hashem* exempts a person under duress." (Bava Kama 28b) But you cannot fool *Hashem* because it says, "*Hashem* knows the thoughts of men, that they are vanity." (Psalms 94:11)

The 'I was in duress' card only works when we aren't thinking about it while committing the error. If we are able to think, we are usually able to stop ourselves or distract ourselves from continuing.

שֶׁבַע יִפּוֹל

The word *sheva yepol*, seven times, has the value of 498 which is the word '*יפתח* *yeftach*' (498), shall open. This is because through falling down, we open new doors in *avodas Hashem*. Without a fall in some way, we cannot justify a gain. But these struggles we go through are not going unnoticed by *Hashem*. *Sheva Yepol* (498) is also the value for '*מנחת* *minchas*,' (498) the meal offering we give to *Hashem* as a *karbon*. Our struggles in life are like *karbonos*, offerings to *Hashem*. They do not go unrewarded and *Hashem* is there throughout all our struggles. "If [whenever] I said, 'My foot has slipped' Your kindness, *Hashem* upheld me." (Psalms 94:18)

Rebbe Nachman teaches us (Likutei Moharan II, 37), "The main purpose of life is only to serve *Hashem* and follow His ways, for the sake of His Name in order to acknowledge Him and come to know Him." So, if the purpose of life itself is to know *Hashem*, why would it matter if we go up or down when He is always there? "If I would ascend to Heaven, You are there; and if I were to make my bed in the grave, You are there." (Psalms 139:8)

To be quite honest, I think sometimes I know *Hashem* better when I am down, then when I am up, because when I am up, everything is going well so I don't really feel like I need Him. When I am down, I am fearless since *Hashem* is beside me, as it says, "Though I walk in the valley of the shadow of death, I will fear no evil for You are with me; Your rod and Your staff, they comfort me." (Psalms 23:4)

As a parent, I can tell you that when my children are doing well in life, I seem to forget to spend much time with them. When they are struggling, I am reminded that they need me and I make more of an effort to give them time, to show them I care and that I walk with them through their struggles. It's not so that *Hashem* isn't with a person when he is up; He is watching from the sidelines, happy to see his success.

"דָּבְקָה נַפְשִׁי אַחֲרֶיךָ בִּי תָּמְכָה יְמִינֶךָ"

"My soul cleaves after You; Your right hand supports me." (Psalms 63:9) As I reflect upon my own *avodas Hashem*, I am reminded of many times that I fell down simply because I was up and didn't know what to do with myself. I was so used to being down, finding *Hashem* through struggles, so when things go well I become bewildered. Does it seem strange that I need support while I am up sometimes even more than when I am down?

The verse, "Your right hand supports me, "has the numerical value of 607, which is also related to the word, ותרא *(vaTayReh* and she saw). "And when the woman saw that the tree was good for food and that it was a delight to the eyes, and a tree to be desired to make one wise, she took of its fruit, and did eat, and gave also to her husband with her; and he did eat." (Genesis 3:6).

When our eyes are open, and we see *Hashem* more clearly, it is then that we need *Hashem* to support us with His right hand all the more. Why did Adam and Chava eat from the *eitz hadas?* It came from pride; they saw that they were close to *Hashem* and therefore they desired not only to be like Him in good deeds but also to be Him. It was the idea of seeking the wrong type of wisdom.

Rebbe Nachman teaches that within wisdom there are stumbling blocks that can enable a person to fall and have to get back up through his faith. "The final letters of the words שֶׁבַע יִפּוֹל צַדִּיק וָקָם *shevA yipoL tzaddik vakaM* spell out the word עֲמָלֵק *Amalek*. For *Amalek* is the stumbling block of the seven wisdoms on which people fall, *Hashem* forbid." (Kitzur Likutei Moharan *19*)

A person falls from his level because he doesn't have balance in his life. He cleaves to *Hashem*, he thirsts for Him, but he really doesn't know how to serve Him with balance. It is like he is drinking water out of the tap but without a filter. Torah is *Chochmah*, but it takes *Binah* and *Daas* to apply it to practical use. So how do you gain perspective so that you won't stumble so frequently and, when you do, you have a structure to fall back on? Well, this is a complicated discussion.

Chazal teach that a person should have one eye on where he is actually holding in life, and one eye on his potential. If we know and understand where we are truly holding in life, then we will study Torah and grow at the proper pace.

The Maggid of Mezeritch, the successor to the Baal Shem Tov, explained this other aspect of *d'vekus*. A Jew must know that, when he is challenged or becomes overwhelmed by the circumstances of life, it is a message that *Hashem* wants him to come closer. Instead of focusing on the hurt, it is more advantageous to become aware of the distance that has come between himself and the Creator. This feeling is *d'vekus*. It can be used to launch a spiritual ascent. In fact, even a seemingly small disappointment can be used in this manner. The sages say that, even if one put his hand in his pocket expecting to find two coins and found only one, it is a message from *Hashem*. "Come closer, come closer", He is urging.

Furthermore, the *maggid* explained that after a person has had spiritual achievements and feels *d'vekus* with *Hashem*, more likely than not he will experience a fall. Nevertheless, he must maintain his *d'vekus* with *Hashem* even if it dips to a very low or weak level. As long he remembers that his spiritual high to *Hashem* has left an indelible watermark on his soul, he has what is necessary to begin his ascent anew, as it is written, "A *tzaddik* falls seven times and rises again." (Proverbs 24:16) He will be able to rise again to an even higher level of *d'vekus*. (Likutei Yekarim) This might be why a *tzaddik* is constantly thirsting for *Hashem*.

Shlomo Hamelech writes in Proverbs (9:1), "With all forms of wisdom she did build her house; she carved out its seven pillars."

The number seven refers to many things, including: The "seven wisdoms", the seven books of the Torah (see Shabbos 115b), and the seven "places" where *Hashem* gave the Torah: (1) from His mouth; (2) face-to-face; (3) from the heavens; (4) at *Har Sinai* [as mentioned in the opening verse of our *parashah*]; (5) in the *Ohel Mo'ed*; (6) in Trans Jordan; and (7) in *Zion*, as it is written (Isaiah 2:3), "From *Zion* the Torah shall go forth." (Toras Ha'minchah)

Rashi, the foremost commentator on the Bible, explains that the seven pillars are a reference to the seven days of creation. The beginning of creation was a time of complete potential that slowly was realized day by day until the creation was complete.

The light of the menorah in the *Bais Hamikdash* also represents the seven wisdoms. The Torah commands Aharon the high priest, "When you light the lamps, toward the center of the menorah shall the seven lamps cast light."(Numbers 8:2)

Why must the six other lights bend toward the center light? According to the Maharal and Rabbi Yonatan Eybeschutz, the seven branches of the menorah in the Holy Temple represent the seven pillars of secular wisdom, knowledge, and science.

Rabbeinu Bachya lists the seven sciences as (1) logic and language (2) mathematics (3) physics and chemistry (4) geometry and trigonometry (5) music (6) astronomy and (7) Divine Wisdom and theology.

The center lamp of the *menorah* represents the light of Torah, which all the other branches face. Rabbeinu Bachya explains that the central shaft of the *menorah* that holds all the branches together is the knowledge of the wisdom of G-d. The other branches of the *menorah* are only the offshoots of that Divine Wisdom. As Psalm 111 states, "*Reishit chachma yiras Hashem* - the source of wisdom is the fear of G-d."

The Vilna Gaon's disciple Rabbi Yisrael of Shklov writes in *Pe'as Hashulchan*, "The Vilna Gaon explained that all secular wisdom is essential for our holy Torah and is included in it." Rabbi Yisrael indicated that the Vilna Gaon had mastered all branches of secular wisdom and knowledge. How did he do this? He did it through his vast knowledge and study of the Talmud, which includes all wisdom.

The Hebrew word for nature, הטבע *haTeva* (eighty-six), has the *gematria* numerical equivalent of *e-l-o-h-i-m* א-ל-ה-י-ם (the name of G-d associated with His kingship over nature). It is the name Elokim that is used throughout the entire first chapter of Genesis in describing the act of creation. The thirty-two times that this name occurs correspond to the thirty-two paths of wisdom. The name Elokim represents understanding. It is nature that gives us an understanding of HaShem, our Creator.

The Rambam explains the verse in *Parshas Ki Sisa* when Moshe asked G-d to, "Show me Your Glory." G-d answered him, "I will make all My goodness pass before you... and you will see My back..." The Rambam explains G-d's answer as follows: If you want to see G-d, it's only by an indirect way, through the study of nature and the natural sciences. (Rabbi Ephraim S. Sprecher, Diaspora Yeshiva in Jerusalem)

We learn in Kabbalah that water is compared to wisdom. The element of water is very soothing to see and listen to. If a person feels a disconnect, visiting a stream or lake can have a relaxing effect. Nature is *Hashem's* hint to us that He is there everywhere we travel. If we can't seem to connect to Him spiritually, there is always the physical presence of nature that surrounds us that can open our heart and draw us closer to Him.

As great as these seven wisdoms are, the common man without Torah guidance will stumble not only through secular wisdom but also Torah wisdom itself. "Whoever is wise, let him understand these things: whoever is prudent let him know them; for the ways of *Hashem* are right and the just do walk in them; but the transgressors shall stumble in them." (Hosea 14:9) That is why it is best to acquire knowledge of Torah from a proper *rabbi*. Then, "Great is the peace of those who love Your Torah, and there is no stumbling for them." (Psalms 119:165)

"Seven times a day I praise You because of Your righteous mandates." (Psalms 119:164) בַּיּוֹם שֶׁבַע is numerically equivalent to 430. This shares the word נֶפֶשׁ *Nefesh* (430), life and soul. A person must go through each day with trials and tests because this is part of life. Rav Kanievsky *shlita* said, "Each day you should complete the study of seven pages of Talmud and then afterwards, you can learn whatever you want." There are seven (7.5) *blats* of Talmud one should study each day in order to complete the Talmud yearly. Through the study of Talmud, one finds life. Instead of experiencing daily trails in life, one fulfils the ups and downs he would normally experience throughout the day through arguments and deep discussions in the Talmud itself. Therefore, it is so important to delve into a page of Talmud every day. One who studies Talmud profusely doesn't have time for life's distractions. Therefore, *Hashem* makes his life easier to accommodate his Torah study, but this is only if he puts his entire heart and life into the study.

Wisdom is something that must be built up with structure. A person doesn't learn calculus without first having gone through basic math and algebra. When it comes to Torah study, it is common for people to skip around and not to create a foundation on which to build further learning. They are simply doing themselves an injustice. While it is important that some of one's study be in subjects he enjoys the most, priority should be in building up his footing.

I once asked the Hornsteipl Rebbe, Rabbi Shalom Friedman, how Rabbi Chaim Vital could become a fitting vessel to learn Torah from the Arizal HaKodesh. He answered with a serious stare in his eyes, "Every day he immersed in the *mikvah* without fail. He began by learning Tanach; he followed this by learning Mishna. Afterward he learned Talmud, and only then did he learn Kabbalah." (Taken from my book, Kavanos Halev)

As the square of seven ($7^2 = 49$), forty-nine denotes the complete cycle within the physical universe. The holiday of *Shavuos* takes place exactly fifty days after the first *seder* of *Pesach*. This parallels the fifty gates of wisdom. The word *Shavuos* means "weeks". It marks the completion of the seven-week *omer* counting. Through this period of counting, the soul must make a deep reflection to receive the proper revelation of Torah on *Shavuos*.

The fifty days of the *Omer* parallel the fifty *Shaarei Binah*. The word *binah* further relates to "*binyan*", building Counting the *Omer* toward *Shavuos* is the process of building, where the Jew builds himself up from the lowly level of an animal up to the spiritual heights of a G-dly being, as he endeavors to transcend the natural and touch the supernatural realm, where he will gain a clearer perception of G-d.

"In the singular form, the word Torah is said to occur fifty times in the Torah." (Rokeach, Deuteronomy 6:7) It is the goal of every Torah scholar to reach the highest level of wisdom and understanding, but the highest level humanly possible is forty-nine gates. It is G-d Who enables a person to make the final leap from forty-nine to fifty. The human being who passed through the full forty-nine gates was Moshe. However, the final fiftieth gate remained beyond his grasp. The secret of this ultimate step would lie within the secret nature of *Yovel* (the fifty-year cycle).

The progression from forty-nine to fifty has, as its precedent, the stepping stone from seven to eight. The soul is likened to the seventh center of holiness within the body that sanctifies the six directions of the physical world toward spiritual pursuits. Through this process the soul can elevate itself, and the body with it, toward perfection. In number terms, the seven is elevated beyond to reach eight, which is synonymous with entry onto the higher transcendental plane. The arrival at fifty similarly marks the entry into this exalted state. (Excerpted from Jewish Wisdom in the Numbers.)

Since complete wisdom can only come from *Hashem's* blessing, you might ask why we can't attain it ourselves; climbing up the previous forty-nine gates wasn't easy either. Why does *Hashem* personally have to give us this exalted state? Didn't all the previous forty-nine gates also require His hand?

I think it might be because *Hashem* wants to remind us that the Torah is a gift. As much as we grasp, the less we know and the more we see the necessity to pray for more wisdom from He to whom wisdom belongs. "Let the name of G-d be blessed forever and ever, for wisdom and power belong to Him." (Daniel 2:20) Dovid Hamelech prays to *HaShem*, "Teach me, *Hashem*, the way of Your statutes, and I will keep them [at every] step. Give me understanding and I will keep Your Torah." (Psalms 119:33)

"Say to wisdom, you are my sister; and call

understanding your woman: that they may keep you from the strange woman, from the alien woman who makes her words smooth." (Proverbs 7:4) Rashi explains "you are my sister" as the idea of "drawing her near to you". Rashi explains further in Song of Songs 7:8, in Hebrew אָחוֹת is an expression of joining (אָחוּי). In order to grasp the Torah, you must not only draw it near to you, you must be joined with it and live it in your very being. You must be sure though to stay clear from the 'alien woman,' who perverts the words of Torah.

Who are those who pervert the words of the Torah? Quite obviously, it would be those who teach Torah for personal gain, honor, and the like. However, we sometimes miss the importance of surrounding ourselves with Torah-minded people. There is a saying, "A person is a composite of the three people he spends the most time with." While friendships can be beneficial as a support system to assist us in getting through the ups and downs of life, the wrong friends can also be a stumbling block. It is the smooth words of the 'alien woman', or so-called friend, that leads us on a wrongful and confused path.

There are seven *Sefiros: Chesed, Gevurah* and *Tiferes* [of *Zeir Anpin*], and *Netzach, Hod, Yesod,* and *Malchus.* [*Malchus* is called] 'seven' because it contains these seven levels. These *Sefiros* are also known as *midos,* emotions that enable us to relate to *Hashem* in terms we understand. All light that comes to us in this world flows through these seven *midos.* We learn from observing *Hashem's midos,* how we too should act. For instance, as *Hashem* has *chesed,* being kind and merciful, so should we be. By perfecting our own seven *midos* throughout our life, we go through the trials of, "A righteous man falls down seven times and gets up." (Proverbs, 24:16)

Lesson 3

"כָּל אַלְמָנָה וְיָתוֹם לֹא תְעַנּוּן
אִם עַנֵּה תְעַנֶּה אֹתוֹ כִּי אִם צָעֹק יִצְעַק
אֵלַי שָׁמֹעַ אֶשְׁמַע צַעֲקָתוֹ
וְחָרָה אַפִּי וְהָרַגְתִּי אֶתְכֶם בֶּחָרֶב וְהָיוּ
נְשֵׁיכֶם אַלְמָנוֹת וּבְנֵיכֶם יְתֹמִים"

*"You shall not oppress any widow or orphan.
If you oppress him, [beware,] for if he cries out to
Me, I will surely hear his cry. My wrath will be
kindled, and I will slay you with the sword, and
your wives will be widows and your children
orphans." (Exodus 22: 21-23)*

There is a special connection between *Hashem* and those who are oppressed in some way. Dovid Hamelech says, "The sacrifices of G-d are a broken spirit; O'G-d, You will not despise a broken and crushed heart." (Psalms 51:19) Many people could fall under this category of being broken-hearted and there is certainly a soft spot in *Hashem's* heart for broken-spirited people. The poor also are held dear in *Hashem's* eyes. "He lifts the poor from the dust; from the dunghill, He raises the pauper, to seat them with princes, and a seat of honor He causes them to inherit, for the pillars of the earth are the L-rd's, and He placed the world upon them." (I Samuel 2:8)

So why does *Hashem* take a special interest in these people? Aren't those who have special needs or other difficulties just as important? You know, many of us in life are going through spats of depression and we know how hard it is to feel trapped in the feeling of absolute loneliness. The

orphan and widow are in total despair; they can try to pop a
pill or talk to a therapist but in the end, they will still feel the
bitterness of exile from their spouse or parent. *Hashem* feels a
special closeness to this *mitzvah* because He too feels the pain
of widowhood and abandonment. He has been separated from
the *Shechinah*, His holy temple, and the closeness to His people
that He desires. Due to our many sins, we have brought this
upon Him. Even though *Hashem* may feel the pain of the poor
or disabled, He does not relate to either in the same way as the
orphan and widow. Though His compassion is endless, He
finds a special relationship, a closer fatherhood towards these
two unique groups of sufferers. Even though the *posukim* start
out as curses, rather than blessings one receives in performing
this act of goodwill, the curses only show *Hashem's* true love
and compassion. It is almost as if *Hashem* is begging us to take
some of the pain off His shoulders. It isn't that He wants to
separate these souls from their precious family; for the overall
good of creation, it has to be this way because souls must come
and go. Especially those that are holy must leave earlier than
usual due to completing their tasks. If you desire to be close to
Hashem, you need to share in what causes *Hashem* pain and find
solutions to help out.

"אַלְמָנָה וְיָתוֹם"

The words *Almana ViyaSom* add up to 590 when you
add two for each word. The number 590 also shares the word
שמרים *sheMuRim'*, watching. Exodus 12:42 speaks of how
Hashem is going to watch over the Children of Israel for all
generations. We know this to be especially true due to the many
strong words *Hashem* uses against those who oppress these two
groups of people, both orphans, and widows. *Hashem* is
specifically 'watching' over them.

Should you choose to hurt these people, it will arouse
Divine wrath on you and your family. Out of all the curses,
some of the strongest language is reserved for this specific
warning.

Divine Wrath, וְחָרָה אַפִּי *Vechara api'*, is the *gematria* 310
which shares the word יכפר *yikapair*, he shall make atonement.

When *Hashem* is upset, we must make atonement in some way through *teshuva* in order to appease His anger. Our rabbis taught: "G-d is angry every day, but how long does His anger last? - A moment." (Avoda Zara 4a) "For His wrath lasts but a moment; life results from His favor; in the evening, weeping may tarry, but in the morning, there is joyful singing." (Psalms 30:6)

Keri (קרי), the wasteful emission of seed, is the same *gematria* (310) and we know that this is something that brings anger to *Hashem;* one must repent for this and make a *yekapair* יכפר (310). Should one be careful to keep himself pure, all the lights of holiness will be upon him.

If a person is careful all his life to minimize the Divine wrath, by being careful to care for the widow and orphan, to watch himself wholeheartedly from sinning with his sexual desires, he will be rewarded in the next world.

The last Mishnah in Tractate Uktzin states: "In the future, G-d will bequeath to each *tzaddik* and *tzaddik* (i.e., each and every *tzaddik*) 310 worlds." What constitutes these 310 worlds? The Alter Rebbe explains in Likkutei Torah: "As Jews, we have 613 *mitzvos* and seven rabbinical laws which equal 620, the same as the *gematria* of *Keser*, crown. As the *Sefirah* of *Keser* represents the world of pleasure, it is thus the ultimate level of reward for doing *mitzvos*. The 310 worlds are exactly half."

So important is this *mitzvah* of caring for the orphan and widow, that *Hashem* will shower you with blessing should you fulfill it. "And the orphan, and the widow, who are in your cities, will come and eat and be satisfied; so that the Lord, your God, (לְמַעַן יְבָרֶכְךָ) will bless you in all the work of your hand that you will do." (Deuteronomy 14:29)

If you take the words, לְמַעַן יְבָרֶכְךָ *LeMaan Yivarchecha* (442), He will bless you, from the *posuk*, you have the same *gematria* as the word, וַיּוֹשִׁיעֵן 'and he helped (rescued) them'. It is so important to be there for these important souls that your reward for this *mitzvah* is quite significant.

Lesson 4

"נַעַר | הָיִיתִי גַּם זָקַנְתִּי וְלֹא רָאִיתִי
צַדִּיק נֶעֱזָב וְזַרְעוֹ מְבַקֶּשׁ לָחֶם"
*"I was young, I also aged, and I have not
seen a righteous man forsaken and his seed seeking
bread."(Psalms 37:25)*

We know that the Talmud in Sota debates this *posuk*. It asks, who was it that could have been both young and old to see so much of life and know that, throughout the generations, there was never such an event. Dovid Hamelech is repeating over these words and we were almost mistaken that they were his original words; but the way he says it, it also shows that he believes he has never seen the righteous forsaken or seeking bread. Rashi explains that it must be the chief angel, not Dovid or anyone else, whom we first think of. The question remains though, why even state the beginning part of the *posuk* at all, "I was young, I also aged?"

Rav Yosef said, "There is a tradition extant, that a diligent young scholar will never become poor." But we see that he sometimes does become poor? Still, we have never seen one so poor that he had to beg his bread from house to house. (Shabbos 151b)

So why did Rav Yosef add that a 'diligent young scholar' will never become poor? What about an older scholar; and if someone is a scholar, obviously, he is going to be diligent or he wouldn't be a scholar.

The Marasha explains, "A Torah scholar has a larger network of admirers than is available to an ordinary person. If the scholar faces deprivation, these patrons will be able at least to support him to the extent that he will not be forced to go begging. Alternatively, he will avoid begging at people's doors by forcing himself to subsist on meager rations."

But this explanation doesn't quench my thirst; I like taking the *posuk* at face value. Also, that might explain an older scholar, as he has more experience living with meager funds, but a young scholar seeks more luxuries. Also, if he is a scholar and righteous man, the original *posuk* says he will not be forsaken and seek bread. If he has to even worry about his sustenance at all, it seems to me he has been forsaken.

Said R. Chiya to his wife, "If you see a man about to beg bread from you, hasten to give it to him; he might at some other time do likewise for your children." She said to him: "Are you cursing your children?"

"Nay; I am simply quoting the verse above, as interpreted by the school of Ishmael, that poverty is a wheel continually turning." (Shabbos 151b)

It must be that Rav Chiya didn't see himself as a scholar, due to his great humility. Otherwise, how could he even fathom that *Hashem* would make him poor and need to worry one day about bread?

This idea that poverty is a revolving wheel works with the general population but the sage, he is above these things, isn't he?

So, let's go back to Rav Yosef's statement: "There is a tradition extant, that a diligent young scholar will never become poor." The Gemara couldn't just leave this statement alone because it knew that many of us would question it. Then it goes so far to admit that there will be a very few who will be poor, but even so, it won't be so bad for them. Rashi explains, they won't have to embarrass themselves seeking the solution.

Rav Yosef's statement still stands on its own merit. For us onlookers, we see the scholar living a simple life; we consider from our own high materialistic standards that he is poor, but he isn't poor at all. Whatever he needs, *Hashem* gives him. We on the other hand, always feel the need to have more.

"נַעַר הָיִיתִי גַּם זָקַנְתִּי וְלֹא רָאִיתִי צַדִּיק נֶעֱזָב וְזַרְעוֹ מְבַקֶּשׁ לָחֶם"

If you take the numerical value of each of the first letters of the *posuk* נהנהגזורצצנומל, you get a total of 487. This is also equivalent to the word, מלאתיו *MeLayseiv*, I have filled him. Not only will the sage be taken care of, but he will also be filled with blessing and sustenance.

The idea of not being poor is being satisfied. There are plenty of rich people out there and if you ask them if they feel satisfied with their life, few will answer yes and if they do, they are lying to you. When we look with materialistic eyes, we need the Gemara to clarify Rav Yosef's words but with a spiritual understanding, we see that his words stand.

Why did he emphasize that a young scholar but not an old one, would not become poor? It is because when a scholar is young, the Torah is still new to him each day, so his progress in learning feels great; he feels filled. The old scholar, he already knows much and realizes that after so many years, he knows nothing. He is sensitive to everything because he wishes he could take back every previous year of his life, so he could use the time more wisely. He also appreciates more the pain of others and he wishes he could support them. Therefore, he may be dissatisfied with his lot only because he doesn't have enough for others. This is why you may see a scholar poor; because he takes his fill and gives it to others.

Rav Chiya told his wife, "If you see a man about to beg bread from you, hasten to give it to him that he might at some other time do likewise for your children." Rav Chiya was telling her, don't think twice about giving charity because it's not so simple. One minute someone can be up and the next minute down. The Gemara explains further, "Rabban Gamliel Bar Rebbe says, whoever is compassionate towards *Hashem's* creatures is shown compassion by Heaven."

As stated above, this older sage especially feels a lacking because he has become more sensitive toward the needs of others.

"The enlightened master knows he lacks nothing and so he prays for his people. But if he lacks nothing, then he knows that in truth they also lack nothing, and if so, for what is he praying?

"He prays they should have open eyes to see and open

hearts to know that in truth they lack nothing. But how can one who lacks nothing pray? Because he knows he himself lacks nothing, but deeper, at his very core, he is his people and he prays as one of them." (Maamar Tefillah L'Mosheh)

Rav Shalom Spitz, *shlita*, once explained that *rachamim* (mercy) really means more than merely feeling bad for another person. Rather, it means actually attempting to fill another's lack.

The sage lacks because he feels for others beyond himself. The original *posuk* says that you will not see "His seed seeking bread." At first glance, you might think this is referring only to his children, but it extends beyond this; anyone who teaches his friend's children Torah is considered as if he gave birth to them. [Sanhedrin 19a]

Not only will the *tzaddik* be lacking nothing; his disciples can also become included in this. How do you become like a child of the sage and therefore feel satisfied with your life?

The merit of those who support the Torah and give money for Torah scholars is very great indeed. This money makes it possible for them to devote themselves to Torah, to give birth to new legal rulings and to open new horizons in Torah. Those who gave the money, therefore, have a share in the Torah which was born and revealed through their help (Likutei Ayzos, Charity # 33)

This seems strange. The sage lacks nothing yet we give him money to support him. It is because for him the wheel is turning faster. As we learned above, "[The] school of Ishmael [taught] that poverty is a wheel continually turning. The *tzaddik* forces the realms of nature to keep having to change themselves. 'The heavens belong to *Hashem*, and the land was given to mankind.'" (Psalms 115:16). This means that mankind, the Jew, is above the constellations. On the other hand, Rabbi Chanina said, "*Mazal* gives wisdom, gives wealth, and Israel is affected by it." Rabbi Yochanan stated, "Israel is not affected by *mazal*." We learn further that through prayer, a Jew can change his destiny. Who is it that perfects the idea of prayer and changes the entire cycle of the world? It is the *tzaddik*. The sages taught, "Who rules over Me? - The *tzaddik!*" (Mo'ed Katan 16b). How does the righteous man rule? The Gemara explains, through his fear of *Hashem*.

Through fear of *Hashem*, a person realizes who he really is. When a person realizes this, he becomes happy with his lot. Reb Zishe was famous for saying that he didn't worry that *Hashem* would ask why he was not like Avraham Avinu, Moshe Rabbeinu, or any other great man. Rather, he worried *Hashem* would ask why he wasn't Reb Zishe.

Only a small minority of people obtain the necessary wisdom to look at the world with objectivity. They take a critical look at each and everything and try to understand everything as it really is instead of accepting the general prevalent outlook. Most people even see themselves as trying to fit into the mold of society even if it means suppressing their own individuality which makes them unique.

Ben Zoma said, "Who is rich? He who is satisfied with his lot." (Ethics of our Fathers 4:1) A few other choice remarks of the *rabbis* come to mind: "One who has one hundred wants two hundred" (Koheles Rabbah 1:34); "One who loves money will not be satisfied with money" (Koheles 5:9) "The more possessions the more worry." (Ethics of our Fathers 2:8)

Chovos Halevavos writes in the introduction to the Shaar Bitachon:

"One who trusts in G-d is secure against mishaps, and his heart is assured against future (potential) bad things. Whatever comes to him from G-d, he will accept with joy and gladness and his livelihood comes to him peacefully, quietly, and happily, as written בִּנְאוֹת דֶּשֶׁא יַרְבִּיצֵנִי עַל מֵי מְנֻחוֹת יְנַהֲלֵנִי (He causes me to lie down in green pastures; He leads me beside still waters).'" (Psalms 23:2)

If you take the first letters of this *posuk* בדיעממי, you have a numerical total of 176. This is equivalent to the word, וַיֹּצִלֵם *VaYaTzeLaim*, and he delivered them. This is because when you put your faith where it belongs, then "*Hashem* is my shepherd, I shall lack nothing." (Psalms 23:1) In fact, even one's enemies will seek peace as it says, "When *Hashem* favors a man's ways, even his foes will make peace with him." (Proverbs 16:7)

In his *perush* on the Chumash, Heichal HaBracha, the Kamarna Rebbe wrote, "The light of Yosef HaTzaddik enlightened all the worlds and all the *Sefiros*. It lit up the world from one end of the world to the other. It was as bright as the sun, but the brothers had no idea that he was such a bright light. As is written in the holy Zohar in parshas VaYeshev, Yosef was everything and was the source of everything. All abundance flowed to the world through him. Yosef was always able to hide his light and his power; 'Yosef was handsome and lovely to see,' has the *rashei taivos* of *yatom* - orphan. The true *tzaddik* is an orphan and he is completely hidden. He is totally concealed, and no one knows anything about him.

While the worthy person conceals himself, *Hashem* is watching over him. From the outside, we may look upon this person as lacking due to observing his simple lifestyle. But what we don't realize is that every humble person is not lacking. We think he is lacking because it is we who are unsatisfied. 'I was young, I also aged, and I have not seen a righteous man forsaken and his seed seeking bread.' Why is this? 'Because the *tzaddik* is the foundation of the world!'" (Proverbs 10:25).

Lesson 5

"וְאַבְרָהָם זָקֵן בָּא בַּיָּמִים וַי-ה-נָ-ה

בֵּרַךְ אֶת אַבְרָהָם בַּכֹּל"

"And Avraham was old, advanced in days,
and the Lord had blessed Avraham with
everything." (Genesis 24:1)

Avraham was always a blessed man, as he knew of *Hashem* in his life, but to receive a full blessing, one must be blessed through his children. Rashi explains that the word בַּכֹּל *Bakol* (52) has the same numerical value as the word בֵּן *ben*, son. It is when the parents live outside themselves, focusing on the good of their offspring, that they complete themselves and find *BaKol*, all.

It is also the same value as the word לִבְּךָ *LeBecha* (52), your heart. When a person does anything in life halfheartedly, he hasn't really done it; however, when you put all your heart into something, then it's לְטוֹבָה *LiTova* (52), for good. וְהִיטַבְךָ *VhaTievaYcha (52)*, and he will do good for you, also shares this value; for when you serve *Hashem* with all your heart, He will bless you as He did Avraham.

בָּאדָמָה *BeDadama* (land) is also adding up to 52. R. Eleazar said in the Talmud Yevamos 63 that a person who doesn't own a home, land, isn't a complete person; therefore, he doesn't have *BaKol*. That is why it is so important to own some form of property. Rav Yitzchok says in the Talmud that a person should divide his money in 3: One-third to invest, one-third in real estate, and one-third to hold onto. (Bava Metzia 42a)

"וַי-ה-נָ-ה בֵּרַךְ (And the Lord had blessed)" has a total *gematria* of 254. This is the same *gematria* of the word צדיקים *tzaddikim*. The sage is blessed with whatever he needs. It is also the same *gematria* of נֶדֶר *neder*. "The L-rd swore to your forefathers, to Avraham, to Yitzchak, and to Yacov, to give them and their descendants after them." (Deuteronomy 1:8)

Rashi asks, why doesn't Moshe just say, "To your forefathers: Why does he [Moshe] further mention Avraham, Yitzchak, and Yacov [when the reference your forefathers clearly indicates them]? [Their names are mentioned to show that] Avraham is worthy [of G-d's oath] by himself, Yitzchak is worthy by himself, [and] Yacov is worthy by himself." (*Sifrei*)

In the same way, any sage who devotes himself to making a strong covenant with *Hashem*, he too could be worthy of a singular blessing from *Hashem*, to have *baKol*.

The word, יחי *vchay* (24), and 'may live' share the same *gematria* as the word ויבאה *VaYeve-Eha*, and he brought her. A person has life when he feels blessed by *Hashem*. But life alone isn't blessed. "*Hashem* fashioned the side that He had taken from the man into a woman, and ויבאה *VaYeve-Eha*, He brought her to the man." Adam was complete only with Chava. Rashi comments, based on the Midrash, that when Sarah was one-hundred, she was like a twenty-year-old regarding sin. The greatness of a twenty-year-old is her physical strength and idealism. G-d said to Avraham: "Whatever Sarah your wife says you shall listen." (Genesis 21:12) Sarah had a way of making Avraham feel young; she was enthusiastic and filled with energy. *Chazal* claims that if the woman isn't happy, the husband won't be either. Sarah also had another name - Yiskah (Jessica), meaning "seer," because she was a prophetess and had the ability to see into the future. Another reason for the name "seer" was that people used to gaze at her beauty (Talmud Megillah 14a). Sarah was exceptionally beautiful, and all other women, by comparison with her, looked like monkeys (Talmud, Bava Basra 58a). As beautiful as Sarah was physically, she was even more beautiful in her nature. She was entirely free of sin, and she was exceptionally modest.

In the merit of Sarah, G-d blessed Abraham with wealth (Midrash on Proverbs 31) and with all other blessings (Tanchuma, Chayei Sarah 4). The greatest blessing for Avraham was that he merited to have Sarah as his wife. As long as Sarah lived, a "cloud of glory" hovered over her tent, and a light burned from *erev Shabbos* to *erev Shabbos*, and her home was full of blessing.

They were partners in every way. In the Torah portion *Lech Lecha*, we are told that when Abraham and Sarah started out for the Land of Canaan, they brought with them "The souls which they made in Haran." (Genesis 12:5) We understand this to mean the people they converted to monotheism. Rashi tells us: "Avraham converted the men and Sarah converted the women." (Ibid.)

To summarize, it was mainly Avraham's family that made him blessed and complete. Sarah his wife and son Yitzchak were his blessings. She brought the *Shechinah* into his home with her devotion to *Hashem* and her desire to raise Yitzchak in the path of *Hashem*. They supported each other in their *chesed* projects and outreach. Alone they wouldn't have been able to accomplish so much but together they changed the world.

The words, זְקַן אַבְרָהָם total *gematria* 405, which shares the word שְׁנֵיהֶם *Shenahem*, two of them. Even though Avraham was old, he was together with Sarah, and therefore his life had completeness. It was the two of them who made the difference and were parents to the Jewish people. If you take the word בְּרַךְ *BayRach*, blessed, it totals 222. All are number 2's because blessing doesn't come alone; blessing comes in pairs.

The Kabbalah teaches that the words "right" and "left" not only describe opposite directions; they also represent two contrasting ideas, perspectives, emotions, and attitudes. The definition of success, on so many levels, is the healthy balance and partnership between two.

Sharing the *gematria* for 222 are the words, יורו *YoRu*, they shall teach and והאיר *VhayEar*, to give light. A person is blessed when he teaches others the light of *Hashem* and Judaism. It was Avraham and Sarah who became this blessed couple that lit up all the future generations.

Sefer Pesukei Torah

Lesson 6

"תָּמִים תִּהְיֶה עִם יְ-ה-וָ-ה אֱ-לֹהֶיךָ"
"Be wholehearted with the L-rd, your Hashem." (Deuteronomy18:13)

Rashi says, "Be wholehearted with the L-rd, your G-d: Conduct yourself with Him with simplicity and depend on Him, and do not inquire of the future; rather, accept whatever happens to you with [unadulterated] simplicity and then, you will be with Him and His portion." [*Sifrei*]

It is the simple faith in *Hashem* that He desires. Sometimes we make our service of *Hashem* so complicated that we actually push ourselves further from *Hashem* rather than closer. Serving *Hashem* simply means doing so happily. If you make your Jewish life complicated with too many *hanhagos*, too much overthinking, you wind up lacking in faith rather than closer.

What does it mean to be תמים *Tamim*, perfect with *Hashem*? תמים *Tamim* (490) has the same *gematria* as וּמַדֹּתֶם *UmaDosem*, you shall measure.

The Klauzenberger Rebbe, Rabbi Yekusiel Yehudah Halberstam, zt"l, offered a priceless interpretation on the biblical narrative describing the patriarch Yacov's dream of the ladder. The Torah tells us that Yacov saw a "Ladder planted in the ground, whose top reached the heavens, and behold there were angels of G-d ascending and going down." (Genesis 28:12) Taught the *rebbe*: If we try to ascend and swiftly transform ourselves into angels, we will fall right back down.

As Maimonides writes in Hilchos Daos (1:2), balanced character traits are ideal (except regarding arrogance and anger). A person must refine himself to be wholehearted with *Hashem*. It is like סלת *SoLes*, fine flour, which shares the *gematria* 490; you should go through all your character traits as you would sift and refine flour until you overcome all flaws.

When you stop trying to be wholehearted, when you stop searching for truth and just give up, that is when you are מתים *MaySim* (490), dead. If a person is trying his best to search for truth, ridding himself of all sophistication which does him no good, then he will be יפת *YaFas* (490), beautiful and goodly in the eyes of *Hashem*.

If you add up the entire *posuk* תָּמִים תִּהְיֶה עִם יְ-ה-וָ-ה אֱ-לֹהֶיךָ, you have a *gematria* total of 1112 = שבתתי *ShabSoSi*, my *Shabbos*.

"And you, speak to the children of Israel and say: 'Only keep My *Shabbosos*! For it is a sign between Me and you for your generations, to know that I, the L-ord, make you holy.'" (Exodus 31:13)

Rashi says, "For it is a sign between Me and you: It is a sign of distinction between us that I have chosen you, by granting you as an inheritance My day of rest for [your] rest."

"כי אות הוא ביני וביניכם: אות גדולה היא בינינו שבחרתי

בכם, בהנחילי לכם את יום מנוחתי למנוחה:"

"To know: [So that] the nations [should know] that I, the L-rd, sanctify you. For it is a sign between Me and you: It is a sign of distinction between us that I have chosen you, by granting you as an inheritance My day of rest for [your] rest."

If you want to know if someone truly is wholehearted about his dedication to *Hashem*, the first thing you look at is their observance of *Shabbos*. All week long a person can make up excuses why he doesn't study Torah, go to synagogue or perform *mitzvos*. It could be his job, his full schedule or the like, but on *Shabbos*, the true nature of a person is revealed. On *Shabbos*, a person's soul becomes *tamim*, whole and perfect.

Shabbos is the light for the entire week; the more a person values the *Shabbos*, the more perfect with *Hashem* he becomes. Yes, *Shabbos* is a day of rest but it is also a day of opportunity. You can't accomplish during the week spiritually what you can on the *Shabbos*. The more you work towards perfecting your *Shabbos* observance, and that goes for all of us, from secular to the most religious, there is always more to improve in our *Shabbos* observance. When we perfect this day, then we begin to serve *Hashem* more devoutly during the week.

Lesson 7

"כִּי אָדָם לְעָמָל יוּלָד וּבְנֵי רֶשֶׁף יַגְבִּיהוּ
עוּף"

"Because man is born for trouble, but flying creatures fly upward."
(Job 5:7)

This *posuk* grabbed my attention due to its interesting wording. Rashi explains it as follows, "Because man is born for trouble." For it is impossible that he should not sin and receive trouble as punishment for sin. He is not like the flying creatures-the angels and spirits-who fly upward and are not of the earthly creatures (other editions read: fly upward so as not to be among the earthly creatures), over whom the adversary and temptation rule.

If man was born for trouble, knowing full well that he would sin during his life, what is really the point of him? It must be, therefore, that even though man most probably will get himself into trouble, he must search for his wings because ultimately, he can fly should he choose to.

"כִּי אָדָם לְעָמָל יוּלָד" (Because man is born for trouble)," is the *gematria* total of 363 which shares the word, הנחש *HaNachash*, the serpent. The evil inclination which is known to be compared to a serpent, will constantly chase a person till his dying day. But what can a serpent do to flying creatures? They rise above the snake and the troubles of this world.

So how do you become a רֶשֶׁף יַגְבִּיהוּ *Reshef YagBeWho* flying creature (*Gematria* 616), unaffected by the troubles of this world? Through התורה *HaTorah* (616): by following and studying the laws of the Torah. בצדקתך *BiTzedKoscha* (616), because of your righteousness you can become untouchable from negative influences.

Job talks a lot about trouble because he had so much. His life was constantly filled with test after test. His only way out of it was to figure out how to perfect his spiritual mindset. "For *Hashem* is the Judge; one He humbles, and one He raises."(Psalms 75:8) Sometimes the only way to come closer to *Hashem* and perfect one's *tikkun* is through humility. *Hashem* pushes you down to the breaking point till the place where the only way out is to start to fly.

The Gemara in Brachos gives two explanations on this *posuk*. Rav Yitzchok said, "Regarding anyone who recites the *Shema* at his bedside before going to sleep, demons keep away from him, as it is stated: and the spirits (*reshef*) soar in flight (*uf*). And the word *uf* is interpreted here as referring only to Torah, for it is stated, 'You close (*hasa'if*) your eyes to it [the Torah], and it is gone.' And the word *reshef* is interpreted here as referring only to demons."

The second opinion is from Raish Lakish who said, "Regarding anyone who engages in Torah study, afflictions keep away from him. As it is stated: and the spirits (*refshef*) sour in flight. And he finds that the word *uf* referring only to Torah, for it is stated elsewhere, 'You close (*hasa'if*) your eyes to it [the Torah], and it is gone.'" (Proverbs 23:5) Rashi explains his opinion to mean, "Suffering (*reshef*) soars (is removed) through the study of the Torah (*uf*)."

Rabbi Yochanan then steps in and exemplifies the words of Raish Lakish and says, even schoolchildren know this (having not learned the book of Job), that they should learn and observe the Torah. Through this, *Hashem* will heal and protect a person. (Brachos 5a)

The Gra explains this *posuk* is leaning towards *mussar*. Your entire life could at any point be over like sparks of fire that just disappear in an instant. He says that if you see you have much good in this world, be wary of it because you will have to pay a price for it either here or in the world above. Why? Man was made for trouble. He isn't like the angels that can fly anywhere in seconds and accomplish their tasks; he must work every moment for his success. The reference to these fiery angels, using the word *Reshef*, is more to scare a person into getting control of his life than to say everything will be okay if you just become more spiritual.

Now let's take the word, עוּף *Uf*, flight. By performing the commandments, a person develops the spiritual wings he needs to soar above physical distractions and troubles. But he must develop himself slowly and build himself a foundation. יוסף Yosef is *Gematria* 156 like the word עוּף *Uf*. Yosef HaTzaddik is known in Kabbalah to represent the *Sefirah* of *Yesod*, foundation. In order to take flight, *Uf* and come close to *Hashem*, you must work on *Yesod*. You must have landing gear or your spiritual flight will be dangerous. You get that from building a solid foundation by following *halacha*, the study of Jewish law. A person must surround himself with a structured Jewish lifestyle built around a synagogue, *rabbi*, and supportive Jewish Torah observant Jews.

It says, "What profit does a man have for all his labor which he toils under (*tachas*) the sun?" (Ecclesiastes 1:3) תחת *Tachas*, under (808) is *KeSef* (808), money in the *gematria* style of *Ayak Bakar*. People are always looking here and there for sustenance but really it is right under their feet. A wealthy person is truly someone who appreciates his family and what he has. Also, if you look at the most successful business people, they usually made it big doing the things they love and enjoy the most. One's potential is something usually he is very talented with, something *Hashem* blesses him with; it is *tachas*, right under him all along. The same is true with everything in life. People always think the grass is greener somewhere else, but many times the things they need to find joy are right there in front of them.

Iyov was a great *tzaddik*. He gave *karbonos* for himself and his children every day. He didn't deserve such a trial, to lose his wealth and children in his lifetime. He suffered so greatly from these tests, but giving up wasn't a choice for him. He was true to *Hashem* through and through. If you want to overcome וּבְנֵי רֶשֶׁף these flying creatures, all of the obstacles that seek to put you down, you should realize that as Rabbi Yehudah said, "*Hashem* created His world only so that [the human beings who populate it] would stand in awe of Him."

(Shabbos 31b) It isn't for us to question His ways because we would be stuck at this *posuk* in Iyov and never understand why man is born for trouble. As Rabbi Schoenes of Baltimore once told me, "Who do you think you are to deserve more than you already have?" And for this, we really have no answer either, because all we know is that we are servants of *Hashem*.

The school of Rav Yannai said, Shlomo HaMelech implies that "it is under the sun where [man] has no profit from labor; but when he labors for that which is above the sun, he indeed has profit from it."

As it says [in the book of Ecclesiastes 12:13], "The sum of the matter, when all has been considered: Fear *Hashem* and keep His commandments, for this is all of man." Rabbi Eliezer explains, "The entire world was created only for the sake of this person [i.e. the person who fears *Hashem* and keeps His commandments]."

But with all that being said, *Hashem* wants us to serve Him with joy, as it says, "So I have praised joy." (Ecclesiastes 8:5) The Gemara explains this to be associated with *mitzvos* performed with joy and through this one is blessed with the *Shechinah* to rest upon him. (Shabbos 30b)

It says in the Talmud, "שהקרבתני תחת כנפי השכינה *HeKRavTani Tachas Kanfei HaShechinah*, You brought me (תחת *tachas*) under the wings of the Divine Presence." (Shabbos 31a)

Why do we say *tachas HaShechinah* instead of beside or above? It is the nature of a parent to hold her children from above to make them feel safe. If we want to feel safe in this world, we need that which preceded the sun; we need the Torah and the *Shechinah* to comfort us. We need to understand our true purpose, accept it and find joy within it. You really can't explain to a non-Jew what having 613 commandments are like. To have complete joy in *Hashem*, to know Him, to fear Him and to perform His will, the commandments with joy. They only have a small taste of this light if they choose to fulfill the seven laws of Noach, but their soul cannot reach that which we can. We should start appreciating the true gift we have been given, the Jewish soul which rises even above the angels. We can only begin to take *Uf,* flight once we appreciate and enjoy the gifts of life that we have been given. To appreciate life, even with its troubles, to focus on the good; that we understand and surround ourselves with positivity. Honestly, I don't understand it all, but I know I am a Jew and you know what, that is enough; and with that, through the performance of the commandments, I can soar! Iyov didn't understand all that was happening, but he knew this and that was enough. Yosef HaTzaddik didn't understand why his brothers went against him, but he hung in there and trusted in *Hashem.* Was it worth it?

"כִּי אָדָם לְעָמָל יוּלָד וּבְנֵי רֶשֶׁף יַגְבִּיהוּ עוּף"

"Because man is born for trouble, but flying creatures fly upward." (Job 5:7)

And that he did.

Lesson 8

"הוֹדוּ לַי-ה-וָ-ה כִּי טוֹב כִּי לְעוֹלָם
חַסְדּוֹ"

*"Give thanks to the L-rd because He is good,
for His kindness is eternal." (Psalms 118:1)*

In its simplest *pshat*, the *posuk* means as following: Each
act of kindness that *Hashem* does with the Jewish people is not
of a temporary nature, lasting merely a day or a year, but its
effects endure forever, as it is said: "The kindnesses of *Hashem*
have not ended nor are His mercies exhausted." (Lamentations
3:22) (Sfas Emes)

As we start to break down the *posuk*, we can see many
other deep wisdom inside it. The entire *posuk* has the *gematria*
of 444, which is the same as מִקְדַשׁ *mikdosh*. When we give
thanks to *Hashem*, we make for him a sanctuary and we too
become holy, מְקֻדַשׁ *MeKodesh*. One of the first things *Hashem*
did for his people was to give us the לוּחֹת *Luchos* (444), and with
this, we were bound to Him for eternity.

If you take the words, 'לְמַעַן יְבָרְכְךָ *LeMaan Yivarchecha*,
(442) He will bless you, from the *posuk* and add one number
for each word, you also come to a total of 444. You have the
same *gematria* as the word וַיּוֹשַׁעֵם and he helped (rescued) them.
By praising *Hashem*, you shower down upon yourself blessing
and salvation.

If you take the first letters of every word of this *posuk*,
you also total 444.

"כִּי שֶׁבַע יִפּוֹל צַדִּיק וָקָם וּרְשָׁעִים יִכָּשְׁלוּ בְרָעָה"
"A righteous man falls down seven times and gets up."
(Proverbs, 24:16).

So how does the righteous man raise himself up after
falling? He does so by giving thanks to *Hashem* for both the
good and the bad. If you take the word טוֹב *tov (seventeen)*, good,

and you use *Atbash*, you get the word נפש *nefesh* (seventeen), soul. When a person has positive thoughts and is always thinking good, his soul is fixed. Also, matching this *gematria* is the word, זבח *zevach*, sacrifice, because one must sacrifice the negativity in his mind and replace it with *tov*.

The word הוֹדוּ לַי-ה-וָ-ה *Hodu LaHashem*, praise *Hashem*, is *gematria* seventy-seven. When are you supposed to praise *Hashem*? Also sharing this *gematria* is the word, בלילה *BaLayla*, in the night. "When I remember You upon my couch, in the night watches I meditate upon You." (Psalms 63:7) And should you fulfill this and praise *Hashem* in the night (which is referring to arising specially at midnight for *chatzos* to pray *Tikkun Chatzos* or to study Torah) then, you have given החסד *HaChesed* (77), mercy from Heaven as it says, "By day, *Hashem* will command His kindness, and in the night His resting place will be with me." (Psalms 42:9)

If you add one for each word of הוֹדוּ לַי-ה-וָ-ה *Hodu LaHaShem*, you get a total of seventy-nine which is the word, האזינו *HaZeiNu*, give ear. It says in the *Zohar*, "*Hashem* joins the souls in *Gan Eden* in listening to the *Torah* that is studied during these hours." (*Zohar* II 46)

"The Torah studied at midnight protects the person in death and in *Gan Eden*" (Chagigah 12) Rebbe Shimon bar Yochai states elsewhere, "*Hashem* descends each night to join those who learn Torah after midnight. They are called the 'Friends of *Hashem*.' All the angels fear them, and they are granted entry through the royal gates and no one can obstruct them." (Zohar 3:92)

"הוֹדוּ לַי-ה-וָ-ה כִּי טוֹב כִּי לְעוֹלָם חַסְדּוֹ"

"Give thanks to the Lord because He is good, for His kindness is eternal." (Psalms 118:1)

Whether it is during the day or at night, the ability to praise *Hashem* is a great blessing. The Midrash in Bereishis Rabbah (chapter 78) tells us that, every day, G-d creates a legion of angels who sing praises to Him and then disappear. If some angels are created just for this simple task of praising

Hashem, it must be far more important than we comprehend. The Midrash mentions that when Moshe spent time studying with G-d over a forty-day period, Moshe could tell what time of day it was when the angels changed singing shifts.

In relation to the recitation of *kedusha* in prayer, the Zohar (Parashas Balak, 190b) explains that the angels cannot open their mouths in praise until the Jewish people gather below to say "*kadosh*". Thus, if the Jewish people throughout the world did not say *kedusha*, the angels too would be forced to refrain from saying it.

Therefore, you can see that, even though *Hashem* enjoys the praise and prayers of the angels, our praise can rise to a much higher level. When Moshe Rabbeinu ascended to *Shamayim* to receive the Torah, the *malachim* objected.

"This secret treasure, which You kept hidden for 974 generations before the world was created, You wish to give to flesh and blood?" they asked *Hashem*.

"Answer them," *Hakadosh Baruch Hu* instructed Moshe Rabbeinu.

"*Ribbono shel Olam*," he replied, "I am afraid that they will consume me with the [fiery] breath of their mouths."

"Hold on to the *Kisei Hakavod*," *Hashem* told him, "and answer them!"

The Piaseczna Rebbe, zt"l, explains that Moshe Rabbeinu feared the *malachim* because he did not realize he was actually greater than they.

The *Kisei Hakavod* is on a higher level than the angels. *Hashem* told Moshe Rabbeinu to hold on to His throne as proof that he, a mere mortal, had the capacity to reach a level that the angels could not.

If praise of *Hashem* is so important, why do we feel awkward sometimes talking to *Hashem* in thanksgiving? Well, I think in general we lack appreciation for life, our blessings, and favors are done to us by others. Parents and teachers try to educate children from a young age to say thank you but learning to be sincere and to really appreciate things takes humility.

For the angels, humility is a gift. They are created to fear *Hashem* and follow His commands. For some, their only job can be to come to life, sing a praise and drop dead. Maybe for us, sometimes it takes a lifetime to realize that we too are created for this purpose, to praise *Hashem* and make His Name known to all the world.

Lesson 9

"רְפָאוּת תְּהִי לְשָׁרֶךָ וְשִׁקּוּי לְעַצְמוֹתֶיךָ"

"It shall be healing for your navel and marrow for your bones."
(Proverbs 3:8)

For generations, doctors understood that the body and soul of a person were connected. When a person became ill, they would look at the person's emotional stability first and only then at their physical body. Many times, he would even go to the sage of his town first for a spiritual answer, before heading down the road of medicine.

It is quite remarkable how today, when a person feels sick, increasing one's Torah study isn't our first reaction. Shlomo HaMelech says, "For they [the teachings of the Torah] give life to those who find them and healing to all flesh."(Proverbs 4:22) It also says: "It is a tree of life to those who take hold of it, and those who support it are fortunate." (3:18)

There is actually a book that has the answers for a sick person, but the sages of Israel endorsed King Hezekiah's action in concealing this Book of Remedies (Pesachim 56a). Hezekiah had sought to instill trust in G-d and faith in the Torah and *mitzvos* as the exclusive Jewish pathway of healing.

It isn't easy to get a person to practice self-reflection. Most people like to keep their minds distracted rather than dwell on the purpose of life. Sometimes it takes illness to bring families together, to make a person wake up and realize how precious life really is. Illness doesn't come randomly, but with the designated purpose of drawing a person closer to *Hashem*.

If you take the last letters of the original *posuk*, you have a *gematria* total of 460.

To a person who is sick in his soul (לנפש *LaNofesh* 460), let him first evaluate his deeds, מעשים *MaAseim* (460). If he

66

can't find anything then let him look to see if he is wasting time; let him look to see if he finds *bitul* Torah, wasting his life not studying Torah (כמת *CaMais 460*, as dead) as a person without Torah is without life. Should he still see nothing, let him assume it is affliction out of love because *Hashem* afflicts those He loves in order to draw them close; they are like his *mikdosh* (ומקדשי *uMikdoshEi* 460, and my sanctuary). This idea is based on the Gemara in Brachos. (Ayin Yaakov 12)

The *gematria* of the last letters of the *posuk* also share the word, מזוזת *mezuzos,* which is 460. "You shall write them on the doorposts of your house and on your gates." (Deuteronomy 6:9) It is known that if someone puts up *mezuzos* on his doorposts for the sake of the *mitzvah* itself, *Hashem* will watch over this person and protect him.

The word, For your bones לְעַצְמוֹתֶיךָ Totals 666.

Interestingly, if you add up the first letter of each word in the *posuk* you also receive the value of 666. Matching the *gematria* total is the word, *TzaaKaso,* their cry. A person who prays in his thoughts alone isn't *yotzei* many of the obligatory prayers. This means that prayer must also be something physical. We should connect our body, most importantly our lips and ears, to the words. As the *posuk* says,

" כָּל עַצְמֹתַי תֹּאמַרְנָה יְ-ה- נָ-ה מִי כָמוֹךָ"

"All my bones will say *Hashem*! Who is like You?" (Psalms 35:10)

According to Rav Chisda, the idea of this *posuk* is to indicate to you that when you pray, you're performing the act with every limb of your body. (Brachos 25a)

And if someone is ill, one should travel to the sage as Rabbi Pinchas suggests, "If one has a sick person in his house, he shall travel to a wise person who shall seek mercy for him, as it is said, 'The anger of a king is the angel of death, but a wise person will atone.'" (Baba Basra, 116b) How is the wise man given this ability? "The will of those who fear Him He fulfills; He hears their cry and delivers them." (Psalms 145:19)

If one cannot travel to the sage, one can ask *Hashem* for help by way of tears, even by himself. "[He is] the Healer

of the broken-hearted and [also] binds up their wounds."
(Psalms 147:3)

When a person is בטל *bitul*, humble, he is saved from
his illness. If you reverse the word *bitul* you have the initial
words of the *posuk*, *Laiv Tohar Bara*, create for me a pure heart.
לטב

The only path to a pure heart is a path of humility.

Great is Torah, for it gives life to its observers in this
world, and in the World to Come. As is stated (Proverbs 4:22):
"For they are life to he who finds them and a healing to all his
flesh." And it says (ibid. 3:8): "It shall be health to your navel,
and marrow to your bones." And it says (3:18): "She is a tree
of life for those who hold fast to her, and happy are those who
support her." And it says (1:9): "For they shall be a garland of
grace for your head, and necklaces about your neck." And it
says (4:9): "She shall give to your head a garland of grace, a
crown of glory she shall grant you." And it says (9:11): "With
me, your days shall be increased, and years of life shall be
added to you." And it says (3:16): "Long days in her right hand;
in her left, wealth and honor." And it says (3:2): "For long days,
years of life and peace, they shall add to you." (Pirkey Avos 6:7)

Joshua b. Levi stated: If a man is on a journey and has
no company, let him occupy himself with the study of the
Torah, since it is said in Proverbs, "For they shall be a chaplet
of grace." (Proverbs 1:9) If he feels pains in his head, let him
engage in the study of the Torah, since it is said: for they shall
be a chaplet of grace to your head. If he feels pains in his
throat let him engage in the study of the Torah, since it is said:
and chains about your neck. If he feels pains in his bowels, let
him engage in the study of the Torah, since it is said: It shall
be a healing to your navel. If he feels pain in his bones, let him
engage in the study of the Torah, since it is said: And marrow
to your bones. If he feels pain in all his body, let him engage in
the study of the Torah, since it is said: and healing to all his
flesh." (Eruvin 54a)

If the reason a person is sick is not his sins, in most
cases it is a lack of Torah study, and even if it is because of his

un-repented sins, the Torah study will fix this up as well. Should a person even be afflicted out of love alone, that *Hashem* wants to draw him close; this too can be helped through the study of the Torah. Not only this, but Torah study is also preventive medicine.

If this is the case, why is there a book of healing that needed to be hidden when the real book of healing is the Torah? Also, the question remains: if the sages of Israel endorsed King Hezekiah's concealment of the Book of Remedies, why does the Talmud itself give explicit details of so many medicines and treatments? This question is addressed by the Maharsha (Rabbi Shmuel Eliezer Aideles 1555-1632) in his commentary on the Talmud:

"Certainly, sanction to heal and to know the remedies for all illnesses has been granted, but it is not proper that they should be revealed to everyone, because of the unworthy people who will trust not in God but in the doctors. Originally it was forbidden to write down the Talmud itself, but because later generations became so forgetful, permission was given to put the oral traditions into writing (Gittin 60a). For the very same reason, the sages were permitted to write down these remedies and reveal them publicly. It was impossible to remember them by heart and they were in danger of being completely forgotten. From their inclusion in the Talmud, you can see that no branch of wisdom is lacking from it. Those who understand the language of the sages will find a true and complete remedy for every illness, and no scoffer will be able to say that the sages of the Talmud lacked healing wisdom." (Maharsha on Gittin 68a)

It was a common practice in the times of the Talmud to practice blood-letting to clean one's blood from ailments. Rav Acha made a prayer before this and Rashi explains it as follows: "People ought not have recourse to medical treatments but should rather pray for mercy."

It says in the Talmud, "The best of physicians are destined to go to hell." (Kiddushin 82a) One of the reasons given for this is that the physician is not afraid of illness and therefore does not turn to G-d with all his heart (Rashi ad loc.).

We do know that the idea of physical remedies does exist in Judaism. Not only did the sages, like the Rambam and even the Talmudic sages, give over countless remedies, but there is also reference to it in the Torah: "As for man, his days are as grass." (Psalms 103:15) "The human body is the tree, the medicine is the fertilizer and the physician is the tiller of the earth." (Midrash Shmuel 52a #4)

A person becomes sick and he starts to think about the things he has done wrong. Some will repent fully for their sins, others might make a less than wholehearted confession, and some will not reflect about their actions at all. The doctors, the medicines, these generally are for people who don't seem to make the connection between their illness, their spiritual growth, and *Hashem*. Of course, there are illnesses that must go through all the above channels but, in general, the first thought of a person isn't that his illness is his own fault. Therefore, he doesn't view the Torah as the true remedy for all things because he doesn't take responsibility for his time on this earth. He studies a little, prays a little, and he feels this is enough. So, what happens with him? The illness reminds him that time itself is valuable. Here he is losing a day of work, study, or adventure so if he is wise he has no choice but to start to evaluate what brought him here and what might prevent him from becoming sicker in the future. The signs are all there; the Torah is the true remedy.

King Hezekiah took the book of remedies away because he wanted people not only to have more faith in *Hashem* but also to open the real book of healing, the Torah. Still, this message doesn't sink into our bones.

Shortly after Shlomo was anointed king, G-d appeared to him in a dream in which He invited Shlomo to make a request for himself. Shlomo answered, "I am but a small child... Give therefore your servant an understanding heart to judge your people..."

His request pleases G-d, who tells him:

"Because you have not requested riches and honor but

only that which would benefit all the people, I will give you not only an understanding heart like none other before or after you... but also riches and honor like no other king in your days."
(1 Kings 3:7-13)

Shlomo HaMelech was the wisest of all men and one of the greatest leaders of the Jewish people. He wrote the Song of Songs, the Book of Ecclesiastes, and the Book of Proverbs. He clearly explains that the key to healing and a healthy life is within the Torah, but we don't receive his wisdom. It is as my wise wife always says, "If I advise you to do something, you won't do it; but when your friends tell you the same thing, you suddenly jump on it as a good idea. "Shlomo was so wise, it is difficult to accept his obvious wisdom. Instead, we suffer throughout our lives, through trial and error trying to figure out the very simple words that he taught:

"The Torah... רִפְאוּת תְּהִי לְשָׁרֶּךְ וְשִׁקּוּי לְעַצְמוֹתֶיךָ it shall be healing for your navel and marrow for your bones."
(Proverbs 3:8)

Lesson 10

"לוּ עַמִּי שֹׁמֵעַ לִי יִשְׂרָאֵל בִּדְרָכַי יְהַלֵּכוּ
כִּמְעַט אוֹיְבֵיהֶם אַכְנִיעַ וְעַל צָרֵיהֶם
אָשִׁיב יָדִי"

*"If only My people would hearken to Me, if
Israel would go in My ways.
In a short time, I would subdue their
enemies and upon their enemies, I would return
My hand." (Psalms 81:14-15)*

If we were simply a rebellious nation, *Hashem* wouldn't keep calling to us and pleading with us to follow the Torah. Therefore, He is constantly focused on our potential. He sees within us a nation that has much good and, like a parent, He says, "שֹׁמֵעַ לִי *Shomya Li*, Listen to me." Why? Because I want to draw you close. These words *'Shomaya Li'* total the gematria 450, which shares the *gematria* of נפשך *Nafshecha*, your soul, and *Shefa*, an abundance of blessing. If you hear me and listen to me, you will be completely blessed beyond your expectations.

Obviously, if I am listening, then I am going to go in the right direction. Why does the *posuk* need to add that Israel should go in my ways? What it means is that you should be like me. As I am kind, you should be kind. As I am truthful, you should be truthful. You are *am Kidoshecha*, a holy nation... Just as I am holy, you should be holy.

שֹׁמֵעַ *Shomaya* is *gematria* 410 which is the same as the word, קדוש *KaDosh*, holy. When we are holy and do the will of *Hashem*, then He will לשכני *LiShaChaini*, dwell among us. As the *posuk* says, "I brought them out of the land of למצרים *Mitzrayim*, that I may dwell among them. I am *Hashem* their G-d." (Shemos 29:46) When *Hashem* dwells among us, we have the משכן *Mishkan*, tabernacle. Incidentally, it was 410 years that the first *Bais HaMikdash* stood. And, because we listened to His will in those years, it had things that the second *Bais HaMikdash* missed out on due to our lower level of *kedusha*. The second *Beis HaMikdash* had no *aron*, no *kapores*, no *keruvim*, no Heavenly fire on the altar, no *urim ve'tumim* for the *kohen hagadol*, no *Shechinah*, and eventually no prophets either.

What makes a person not listen? It is stubbornness, which shares our *gematria* 410. It says in, "Remember Your servants, Avraham, Yitzchak, and Yaakov; look not to the stubbornness of Your people." (Deuteronomy 9:27)

A person is stubborn because he has pride. Stubbornness is the opposite concept of listening. The entire idea of listening is to humble yourself and realize that you can learn from others. "Ben Zoma would say: Who is wise? One who learns from every man." (Pirkey Avos 4:1) "Let the wise man hear and increase learning. The understanding man shall acquire wise counsels." (Proverbs 1:4-5) If you can't humble yourself to listen to other people, how will you do so with *Hashem*?

"If your wife is short, humble yourself and bend down and listen to her." (Baba Meziya 59a) A person's wife is a reflection of the *Shechinah*, Divine Presence. Through her, a man learns to greet the *Shechinah* and appreciate Her. She is his miniature *Bais Hamikdash*. Through her, he sanctifies himself and becomes holy.

"בִּדְרָכַי יֵהָלְכוּ"

"Go in my ways"

This is *gematria* 307, which shares the name רבקה Rivka. we learn that Rivka is the daughter of Bethuel, and the sister of Lavan (also known as the conniving, greedy father of Rachel and Leah, who switched Rachel for Leah and extorted Yaakov for all he was worth). Bethuel is not a nice guy either, as related in the Midrash:

"...[Bethuel] was evil and tried to prevent Rivka from going with Eliezer, and he tried to poison [Eliezer]." (Rashi, Genesis 25:51)

So, we see that Rivka comes from a rather despicable

family background:

Since G-d knew that the Jewish people would be spread out among the nations when in exile, and typically one is influenced by his surrounding culture, He wanted our matriarchs and patriarchs to be among evil people and withstand their influence. In this way, their descendants will have the strength to hold onto their religion even in exile, since "The acts of the ancestors are a sign for their descendants." (Tiferet Tzion)

If we want to know how to go in the ways of *Hashem*, we should read stories of our ancestors. What they faced was nothing like the personal confrontations we have today in our service of *Hashem*. When we pray, we say, remember the merit of our forefathers; but these words in prayer are not just for *Hashem* but also for us as a remembrance. If we think about what they went through and how they persevered, we too will realize that we can overcome our personal exiles.

So how do we return to a better path in

"בִּדְרָכָיו יֵלֵכוּ"

We should cherish every new day at its inception. When is that? הַבֹּקֶר *HaBokair*, in the morning. *HaBokair* shares the *gematria*

"בִּדְרָכָיו יֵלֵכוּ"

To go in the ways of *Hashem*, a person must constantly work on how he starts each day. When you wake up in the morning, think of a *posuk* in the Torah to start your day. Make sure to have only positive thoughts and believe that the day will be successful. To go in the ways of *Hashem*, you must be ready to accept the truth of life, that we are servants of *Hashem* and our goal is to serve Him. It is in the morning that you grab positivity and creativeness for the rest of your day.

"מוֹדֶה אֲנִי"

"I give thanks"; this is the prayer we say first thing in the morning. To go in *Hashem's* ways, we must be thankful. If we don't appreciate what we have, we can't be humble enough to listen to *Hashem*. מוֹדֶה אֲנִי is the *gematria Mispar Katan* twenty-six, the same as the name of *Hashem*, YKVK.

So, if we do the will of *Hashem*, the next *posuk* tells us,

"כִּמְעַט אוֹיְבֵיהֶם אַכְנִיעַ וְעַל צָרֵיהֶם אָשִׁיב יָדִי"

"In a short time, I would subdue their enemies and upon their enemies, I would return My hand."

It would seem perfectly sufficient if the *posuk* started out with, 'I would subdue their enemies.' Why add the word, כִּמְעַט *Kimat*, in a short time? If you scramble the letters of the word *Kimat*, you have the word כטעם *KTaAm*, as the taste. "[The Manna they] made cakes of it: and the *KTaAm*, taste of it, was like the taste of oil cake. And when the dew fell upon the camp in the night, the manna fell upon it."

After a person completely accepts the severity of *Hashem*, He sends salvation in a short time, even if it goes beyond *teva*, the normal way of the world. He will bring salvation even to your doorstep; this is because His only wish is for you to listen to Him and go in His ways.

I think the problem for many of us is that we don't believe in miracles anymore. We are like stubborn children, hoping our Father will simply reach out to us and fix things for us. We sin to get more attention from Him, thinking He won't otherwise notice us. If we properly believed in repentance, in the numerous miracles that befell our people after they corrected their ways, we would simply behave as proper Jews.

That is why we say, "Remember I took you out of *Mitzrayim*," many times a day in prayer. Because if only we would remember and believe in the power of *Hashem's* salvation, we would stop rebelling and return to him. "Return to me, and I will return to you", says *Hashem*. (Malachi 3:7) And your salvation, it will come quickly, so don't worry. I know you're in pain and hurting so just come back.

Lesson 11

"לַיְּהוּדִים הָיְתָה אוֹרָה וְשִׂמְחָה וְשָׂשֹׂן וִיקָר"

"The Jews had light and joy, and gladness and honor." (Esther 8:16)

If you take the first letter of every word, you get the *gematria* for the word אמחה *EmChe* (54), I will blot out and destroy. When a person has joy in his לבבך *Livavecha*, heart, which is also total to fifty-four, having faith that *Hashem* will help him, his enemies, as we see in the story of *Purim*, slip away.

This theme of concealment is found in the very name of the heroine of *Purim*. The name Esther derives from the root *str*, which in Hebrew means hidden. In the *Torah* (Dt. 31:18), God says to Israel, "I will surely hide *(hastir astir)* My face from you..." The sages see this Hebrew phrase as a subtle suggestion of the hiddenness of God during the time of Esther.

Take Esther herself. No one except Mordechai knows who she really is. Even King Ahashverosh is kept in the dark. *"Ein Esther magedet moledetah,"* says the Megillah in 2:20. "Esther did not reveal her origins..." This is the theme of the day: nothing is revealed.

We learn in Kabbalah that *Hashem's* names are put into attributes such that we can understand how He deals with the world, but during *Purim*, we witnessed a miracle that transcended any such attribute. This type of miracle relates more to G-d's essence than to any of His specific attributes. And *Hashem's* essence has no name. Therefore, *Hashem's* name is not mentioned in the *megillah*.

The aim of *Purim* was achieved without any natural laws being broken. Vashti was ousted. Esther was chosen. Mordechai overheard a plot. Achashverosh couldn't sleep. Esther found favor in the king's eyes. Everything went according to *teva*, the natural order of events. There was no big flood, river splitting or plagues. In a way, the miracles were completely hidden. Which is why we wear costumes, hide our face, hide from reality, and drink until we don't know the difference between Mordechai and Haman. It is because reality hides the simple greatness of *Hashem* and the Torah. Life itself and its distractions cover over the daily miracles of life itself according to *teva*, the natural order of events. If only we took a few minutes a day to step outside ourselves and notice all our blessings.

During *Purim*, everything is reversed. Let us take the *gematria* of לבבך *Purim* in *Atbash*. The total comes to 139, which shares the word כטעם *Ktaam*, as the taste. "And the taste of it was like the taste of oil cake." (Numbers 11:8)

Sometimes in life, we must slow down to think and reflect. Rav Simon Schwab (1908-1995) related how he once spent *Shabbos, Parshas Be'Shalach,* in the home of the Chofetz Chaim (1838-1933). They were discussing the *manna*. The *Medrash* relates that the *manna* would taste like whatever a person would desire. If you thought fried chicken, it would taste like fried chicken; if you thought macaroni, it would taste like macaroni, etc. So, they asked the Chofetz Chaim, "what if someone ate the *manna* without thinking about anything - then what would it taste like?" The Chofetz Chaim responded, "if you did not think - then it had no taste! [*oib me'tracht nisht; es haat ken ta'am nisht.*]"

It's the same thing with *Purim*. People go through life without אוֹרָה וְשִׂמְחָה light and joy but they don't have to. Life can taste whatever way you want it to. There are always hidden miracles and *Hashem's* blessing right before us, but we should decide that we want to taste it.

"לַיְּהוּדִים הָיְתָה אוֹרָה וְשִׂמְחָה וְשָׂשׂן וִיקָר"

Lesson 12

"מִי הוּא זֶה וְאֵי-זֶה הוּא"
"Who is he, and where is he."
(Esther 7:5)

In its simple meaning, Rashi says, and King Ahashverosh said, and he said to Queen Esther: Wherever it says, "and he said, and he said," twice, it is to be expounded upon, and the Midrashic interpretation of this is: Originally, he would speak to her by messenger, but now that he knew that she was of a royal family, he spoke to her personally.

It is the same with us; when we start to seek *Hashem*, asking who He is, Where is He, we no longer become a stranger. *Hashem* extends us his hand so that we may enter before Him. King Dovid cries out, "Who is He, this King of Glory? *Hashem* of Hosts, He is the King of Glory. *Selah*." (Psalms 24:10)

"מִי הוּא זֶה וְאֵי-זֶה הוּא"

This *posuk* adds up to 115, which is the same *gematria* as הנני *HeNaiNe*, here am I. That *Hashem* did test Avraham, and said to him, "Avraham: and he said, Here I am!" (Bereishis 22:1) When a person looks for *Hashem*, he will always find Him. The most important thing is to always be looking for an attachment.

How do we find *Hashem*? We are tested, נסה *NeSaw*, as we see Avraham was tested to prove his devotion to *HaShem*.

When we overcome the tests that we confront in our life, then "they shall offer sacrifices of righteousness: for they shall suck of the abundance of the seas, and of treasures hid in the sand" (Devarim 33:19). The word טמוני *Timunai*, treasures, also adds up to the words הנני *NeNaiNe* and נסה *NeSaw*. It is also written in scripture: He girds the afflicted in his affliction! - [The meaning is that] as a reward for his affliction He will deliver him from the judgment of *Gehennom*.

78

What, however, is the explanation of the scriptural text, "The angel of the L-rd encamps round about them that fear him, and He girds them?" [The meaning is that] as a reward for those who fear Him, He will deliver them from the judgment of *Gehennom*. (Yevamos 102b)

"וְאֵי-זֶה הוּא" (41)

"And, where is he?"

HaShem can be found in the הָאֹהֶל *Ohel*, the tent, (41) in the *bais midrash*, learning the Torah. This is the Torah [law]: If a man dies in a tent, anyone who enters the tent... becomes impure for seven days. "Taking the part of the verse, the Talmud comments: "This is the Torah - if a man dies: "Torah is only acquired if a person kills himself over it" (Brachos 63b). Torah knowledge cannot be acquired passively. We must work very hard to acquire it, even to the extent of killing ourselves in this world, overcoming all materialistic desires.

Hashem hides Himself, only so much that we should go looking for Him. But when searching, we find He is right there. Just as when you play hide and seek with your child, you want him to be able to find you easily. *Hashem* has no intention of making it difficult to find Him. He, therefore, hides in plain sight and to find Him, you just should ask the question.

"מִי הוּא זֶה וְאֵי-זֶה הוּא"

"Who is He and where is He in my life?"

When you look at your life and realize it is the tests that *Hashem* has put you through that helped you to find Him, you will no longer fear such tests if they happen again because you will realize that is where he is. Mordechai and Esther saw a challenge, that they were put in a position to help all of Israel. They rose up only because they asked the question, where is *Hashem* in this situation and what do I need to do?

Lesson 13

"חָנֵּנִי יְ-ה-וָ-ה כִּי אֻמְלַל אָנִי רְפָאֵנִי

יְ-ה-וָ-ה כִּי נִבְהֲלוּ עֲצָמָי"

"Be gracious to me, O'L-rd, because I languish; heal me, O'L-rd, because my bones are frightened." (Psalms 6:3)

In Rashi's simple interpretation, *Umlal* means, devastated, and poor in strength. A person is crying out how feeble he feels, confused and to the point of fright. There are many levels of sickness, but nothing beats preventative medicine.

Sharing the same *gematria* as the entire *posuk*, 1036 is the phrase

"וְנִשְׁמַרְתֶּם מְאֹד"

"Be very careful, guard yourself." (Deuteronomy 4:15)

A person should be careful to take care of both his physical and spiritual wellbeing. It isn't enough to just run to *Hashem* or the doctor when we don't feel well. We must practice healthy eating, exercise, and spiritual meditation for our souls.

But should we be sick, we must call out,

"רְפָאֵנִי יְ-ה-וָ-ה"

and not rely on the doctor alone.

These two words, *totaling* 363, are *gematria* המשיח *HaMoshiach*. The complete healing of the world is from the coming of the *Moshiach*.

If you take the first words of the *posuk*,

"חָנֵּנִי יְ-ה-וָ-ה כִּי אֻמְלַל אָנִי"

You come to a total of 336, which shares the *gematria* הרפאים *HaRofeim*, the physicians. When a person is ill he goes to the physician, viewing him as an agent of *Hashem* to enable healing, but a doctor alone has no power; it takes *Hashem's* graciousness to allow the healing to take place.

It is important that we make *Hashem* One, believing in complete faith that it is He who heals us. So, let us add one to 336 and we total 337, which

Shares the word

"וְנִרְפָּא"

VNearPa, and it is healed because before *Hashem* gives the illness to a person, way before we began to pray for salvation, He already created the antidote. As it says, "I will answer them before they even call to me." (Isaiah 65:24) *Chazal* says that the same energy that brings the disease is the same energy that heals it. That is why you see in many cases that the antidote for a snake or scorpion bite can be made from the same poison that is admitted to causing harm.

We also learn this from a Rashi, "כָּל הַמַּחֲלָה אֲשֶׁר שַׂמְתִּי בְמִצְרַיִם לֹא אָשִׂים עָלֶיךָ כִּי אֲנִי יְ-הֹ-וָ-ה רֹפְאֶךָ"

"All the sicknesses that I have visited upon Egypt I will not visit upon you, for I, the L-rd, heal you." (Exodus 15:26)

I will not visit upon you: And if I do bring [sickness upon you], it is as if it has not been brought, "for I, the Lord, heal you." This is its Midrashic interpretation see Sanhedrin 101a, Mechilta. According to its simple meaning, [we explain:] "For I, the L-rd, am your Physician." and [I] teach you the Torah and the *mitzvos* in order that you be saved from them [illnesses], like this physician who says to a person, "Do not eat things that will cause you to relapse into the grip of illness." This [warning] refers to listening closely to the commandments, and so [Scripture] says: "It shall be healing for your navel." (Proverbs 3:8)

We also see this from the story of King Chizkiyah; there was a book of healing from *Hashem* that already existed from the time of Adam, which King Chizkiyah chose to hide so that people would pray to *Hashem* and not rely just upon remedies.

Furthermore, the Torah is the only true help against sin

and that too *Hashem* created before He created its adversary.

The *rabbis* taught: The Torah says, "וְשַׂמְתֶּם *Visamtem*, And you shall place these words of Mine on your hearts and on your souls..." (Deuteronomy 11:18). You can also read that as "שָׂם-תֹּם *sam tom*," a perfect medicine. The Torah is the perfect medicine.

The *rabbis* gave a parable, comparing it to a man who wounded his son, so he put medicine and a bandage on the wound. He told his son, "As long as you keep the bandage with the medicine on your wound, you can eat with pleasure, drink with pleasure; you can wash with hot water or cold water, and you don't have to worry about it. If you take off the medicine, it will get gangrenous."

Likewise, *Hashem* has told Israel, "My children, I have created the Evil Inclination, and I have created the Torah as an antidote against it. I wrote in My Torah: 'If you do good, you will be more powerful. If you do not do good, sin awaits crouching at the door; it desires to control you, but you can overpower it.'" (Genesis 4:7)

"As long as you are engrossed in the Torah, you will not be controlled by the evil inclination. Therefore, the Torah says: 'If you do good, you will be more powerful'. But when you are not engrossed in the Torah, you will be under the control of the Evil Inclination, as the verse continues, 'If you do not do good, sin awaits crouching at the door'."

"Not only that, "*Hashem* said, "but the Evil Inclination will spend all its time and energy trying to make you sin, which is why the verse says, 'it desires to control you.'"

"If you want to, you can overpower the evil inclination, as it says, '...it desires to control you, but you can overpower it.'" (Kiddushin 30b)

Refa'einu veneirafei. Heal us and we will be healed. Heal us - for if You heal us, we will certainly be healed. The Hebrew root for healing, רפא (*RePh'A*) is a rearrangement of the letters of the word פרא (*PeR'E*), meaning "wild". So long as there is no healing, the elements within one are wild and out of joint. The body, the mind, the soul, the very world is "desolate and formless"- like the earth before the revelation of G-d's light (Genesis 1:2). It is the light of spirituality that brings order to the elements. True healing, רפואה (RePhu'Ah), turns פרא (PeR'E), wildness, into פאר(Pe'ER), which means beauty and harmony, the true beauty of G-dly revelation. (Wings of the Sun, Chapter 1)

"A joyous heart is good medicine, whereas a broken spirit dries the bones." (Proverbs 17:22)

The Rambam stated, "The physician should make every effort to see that everyone, sick and healthy alike, should always be cheerful, and he should seek to relieve them of the spiritual and psychological forces that cause anxiety. This is the first principle in curing any patient." (Rambam, Hanhagas HaBri'us 3:13-14)

"There was a certain sick man whom a great and famous Jewish doctor had given up all hope of curing. The man was unable to speak. The Baal Shem Tov was visiting his town and was asked to come to see him. The Baal Shem Tov told them to prepare the invalid a meat soup and said that as soon as he ate it he would start to speak. They gave him the soup and he recovered. The doctor said to the Baal Shem Tov, 'How did you cure him? I know that his blood vessels were irreparably damaged.'

"The Baal Shem Tov replied, 'Your approach to his sickness was physical but mine was spiritual. A person has two hundred and forty-eight limbs and three hundred and sixty-five veins and arteries, corresponding to the two hundred and forty-eight positive precepts of the Torah and its three hundred and sixty-five prohibitions. When a person fails to carry out a positive *mitzvah* the corresponding limb is damaged, and when he contravenes a prohibition the corresponding blood vessel is damaged. If he contravenes many prohibitions many blood vessels become damaged. The blood does not flow, and the person is in danger, but I spoke to his soul and persuaded her to repent, and she undertook to do so. This way all his limbs and blood vessels were repaired, and I could heal him.'" (Shevachey HaBaal Shem Tov #125)

"The main thing is faith! Every person must search within himself and strengthen himself in faith. For there are people suffering from the most terrible afflictions, and the only reason they are ill is because of the collapse of faith." (Likutei Moharan 2, 5:1)

Lesson 14

"חִזְקוּ וְיַאֲמֵץ לְבַבְכֶם כָּל הַמְיַחֲלִים
לַי-ה-וָ-ה"

"Strengthen yourselves, and He will give your heart courage, all who hope to the L-rd." (Psalms 31:25)

Rashi says, "Strengthen yourselves, and He will give your heart courage."

Dovid HaMelech says, as you see He did for me, to save me because I hoped for Him.

He is reminding us: look at the example of my life and you can see all the troubles I went through, yet *Hashem* saved me, and He will do for you what He did for me.

Now that is a great thing coming from Dovid HaMelech; *Hashem* lifted him up to a great stature. He became a king, powerful, wealthy; he was honored around the world and had great wisdom in Torah.

How do you strengthen yourself and find the courage to handle every obstacle in your life? Through the Torah! If you add up the numerical value of the entire *posuk*, you come to 611, which shares the word Torah.

We learned in the Talmud, "Torah scholars tend to be somewhat feebler than the general population because their studies sap their strength" (Nedarim 49a). So how can it be that the Torah will weaken a person? Its study can be very intense. A scholar generally sleeps less and eats less because he is occupied with his studies. It says in the Talmud, "a scholar eats his meals later than the normal population" (Shabbos 10a, Pesachim 12b), but we see from Rav Yochanan that if one has *koach*, he should use it for the Torah. Rav Yochanan called out to Raish Lakish, who was then a highwayman devoid of Torah, "Your strength belongs to the Torah!"(Bava Metzia 84a) It further says in the Talmud that Rav Yochanan took this strength, this potential he noticed in Raish Lakish and "Made him into a great man." How does he regain his strength and also become great in Torah? It's difficult to imagine that he should have to suffer because of his devotion to *Hashem*. Rav lived only forty years and studied Torah day and night, but Abaya lived for sixty. The Gemara explains that it was because Rav only involved himself in learning, but Abaya involved himself also in other *mitzvos* like *gemilas chasadim*, kindness to others. (Avoda Zara 19b)

Torah study itself is great but to add the performance of the commandments, especially kindness to others, is what returns one's strength that is otherwise sapped by the fatigue of learning. How do we get from Torah to the commandments? As you recall, the *posuk* totaled 611 as with the word תורה Torah; just add two and you have the 613 commandments. Why does the word *Torah* only add up to 611 instead of the sum of the *mitzvos*, 613? *Hashem*, not Moshe, spoke the first two commandments directly to the Jewish people. "I am the *Hashem*, your G-d," and, "You shall have no other G-ds before Me. "Only after *Hashem* concluded the first two commandments did the Jews, fearing the heavenly voice, beg Moshe to intercede and continue the transmission of the Divine word.

Moshe did indeed command us the sum of Torah, 611 laws. The other two are in a category all by themselves, having been a legacy from the lips of *Hashem* Himself.

"וַיַּרְא אֱ-ל-הִ-י-ם אֶת הָאוֹר כִּי טוֹב"

"And G-d saw the light that it was good." (Bereshis 1:4)

This *posuk* adds up to a total of 613 because it is the *mitzvos* that enlighten a person's being. Any strength that is utilized in Torah study, returns with the light of the *mitzvos*.

The Hebrew word *yirah* means both "to fear" and "to

see. "The essential choice of life is to open our eyes to available opportunities, and to fear the consequences of avoiding that reality. Therefore, we must strengthen ourselves in fear of *Hashem*. The word, *yiras* totals 611. If you add up the last letter of each word of the original *posuk*, you also get the word *aray*, (211) you fear.

"He gave food to those who fear Him; He is ever mindful of His covenant (ברית)." (Psalms 111:5) The Torah is the covenant between us and *Hashem*, yet the word ברית *bris* only adds up to 612. It is because to keep the covenant with *Hashem*, you must take the first step; you must have *emunah*, faith in one *Hashem*. When you do this, you have 613.

"כָּל הַמְיַחֲלִים לַ יְ-ה-וָ-ה"

"All who hope to the L-rd"

Is numerically equivalent to 249, which shares the word הצדקים *HaTzaddikim;* because, when you believe in *Hashem* wholeheartedly, you become righteous. And through this, *Hashem* will show you ארחם *Arachaim* (249), mercy and ואברכך *VaAvaReChecha,* (249) and He will bless you.

87

Lesson 15

"בִּרְכַּת יְ-ה-וָ-ה הִיא תַעֲשִׁיר וְלֹא יוֹסִף עֶצֶב עִמָּהּ"

*"The blessing of the L-rd will bring riches,
and toil will add nothing to it."
(Proverbs 10:22)*

Rashi explains, "One need not toil to gain wealth, for it is enough with the blessing that He blesses him. "People think if they work harder, longer hours they will become wealthy, but this isn't the case. They might make more money, but wealth needs a special blessing from *Hashem*.

In the ideal world, the world of Adam before he sinned, a person wasn't meant to toil to have food. Adam was positioned in the Garden of Eden where food was bountiful. Man's purpose wasn't to toil in agriculture, but rather to bask in the joy of Torah study.

And to man He said, "Because you listened to your wife, and you ate from the tree from which I commanded you saying, 'You shall not eat of it,' cursed be the ground for your sake; with toil shall you eat of it all the days of your life." (Genesis 3:7) It was the curse that *Hashem* gave Adam after he partook from the forbidden tree: he would have to sweat in order to sustain himself. This means that ideally, we shouldn't have to toil for our food. In an ideal state, we learn Torah and *Hashem* provides for us.

Shlomo HaMelech is reminding us here: you must understand that blessing, especially for riches, comes only from *Hashem*. Your toiling may not directly increase your wealth, so don't set all your energy on toiling for more than what is necessary to support yourself humbly.

"וְלֹא יוֹסֵף עֶצֶב עִמָּהּ"

"and toil will add nothing to it."

These words share the same numerical value as the word עֵת *Ais*, time (470). If you toil for wealth you're just wasting your time because, even if you were to make more money, you had already been blessed this amount on Rosh Hashanah. (see Rosh Hashanah 1:3, 16a) You would have been given it anyway, so your toil was for nothing. I'm not saying you shouldn't work hard, that you shouldn't toil in work. Adam's curse was that he should toil the land. We know that people who work sometimes study Torah better working half a day, because it gives their life organization and purpose. Otherwise, they would waste much of their day in sin. Should you be one who needs to feel he is accomplishing something with his work, it's understandable--as the word כנפשך *KNafShecha*, for your own pleasure, also shares the total 470. When you toil more than necessary for your basic needs, do it for yourself, because you want to feel accomplished, not because you think that your hands can become like a golden calf.

There are many successful people in business and most of them don't work that hard. Some were blessed with an inheritance; some became very lucky and had instant success, while others were in the right place at the right time. A good businessman values his time so, to make sure he has more of it, he creates a staff around him of hard-working people. If he is smart, he tries to make them a mirror of himself so that eventually he doesn't even have to run his business. He also can accomplish more in a shorter period of time because he knows how to stay focused and motivated. A person really doesn't have to destroy his potential to become a Torah scholar in order to make a living. He should just use his time and energy wisely.

If wealth is your desire, recognize that this comes from *Hashem*. Your hard work might be appreciated, but you only need to form a vessel for His blessing to enter. Let the study of Torah be your obsession. Make work secondary and, if you want to become rich, the Torah tells us how to accomplish this.

"Be careful to tithe ('*Asser Te'asser*'- lit., 'tithe, you shall tithe') all the produce of your seeds that come out of the field every year." (Deuteronomy 14:22)

R. Yochanan said: What is meant by the double expression, "tithe you shall tithe"? It should be read as "Tithe ('*Asser*') so that you will become rich (*Titassher*)"...

R. Yochanan's nephew asked him, "How do you know that tithing makes one rich?" He replied, "Go and try it, and you will see for yourself!"

"But," the nephew protested, "is one permitted to put *Hashem* to a test?" R. Yochanan answered, "I have a tradition from R. Hoshayah that in this one case it is permitted to test *Hashem*, as it says (Malachi 3: 10), 'Bring all your tithes to the storage house, and test me by this - see if I do not open up the windows of the heavens and pour out upon your endless blessings!'" (Taanis 9a)

In Kesubos 66b, a popular saying of the people of Jerusalem is recorded: "The way to 'salt' (preserve) money is to diminish it (give charity)."

In Betzah 15b the Gemara says, "Rav Yochanan... said: If someone wants to ensure that his property will remain his, let him plant an *Adar* (lit., a type of cedar tree). What is an *Adar*? As it says in Psalms (93:4): '*Hashem* is mighty (*Addir*) on high.'" Rabbenu Chananel explains that the Gemara means to interpret Rav Yochanan's "*Adar*" as a pun. He didn't mean that we should plant cedars, but that we should "plant" our money with the Mighty One on high (*Addir*). Giving charity is like depositing your money in a celestial bank, where it is safe from worldly burglars or accidents. It is considered as if one has given his money to the Mighty One on high for safekeeping, as it says (Tehillim 85:12) "Charity (*Tzedek*) peers out from the heavens." (See also Bava Basra 10a.)

Rav Menachem Azarya ("The Rama," for short) of Pano points out that the word *Tzedakah* - Tzadi, Dalet, Kuf, Heh, when transposed into its *Atbash* equivalent, comes out to be the exact same word spelled backwards - Heh, Kuf, Dalet, Tzadi.

This may be meant to demonstrate that whatever charity a person gives is bound to return to him in the opposite direction, as "charity" from *Hashem*!

Rabbi Avigdor Miller zt"l explained that the *aron's* constant readiness for travel reminded the *bnei Yisrael* that they too might be asked to leave their encampment at a moment's notice. Due to this lack of permanence, the Jewish people never became attached to their material surroundings and could focus solely on the study of Torah. This is an important lesson for us as well. If we are to succeed in *limud haTorah*, we must first recognize the transitory nature of this world. "One must consider Torah study to be his main occupation and work, as the means to achieve that goal." (Brachos 35b) This does not depend so much on the amount of time one devotes to learning, as on one's attitude towards learning. One who anticipates the moment that his work will be finished so that he can go learn, and whose every spare moment is devoted to *Torah* study, demonstrates that this is his main focus. On the other hand, if one learns many hours a day but is preoccupied with what he will do after his learning *seder* (session), and he rushes home when he is done, then he shows that Torah learning is not as important as it should be.

For those whose dream it is to study Torah full time, this is also possible through *emunah*, faith. There are no limits to the blessing brought down from Heaven for those who fear *Hashem* and have faith in Him. Rav Aharon Rutt would say over that, if a person reaches into his pocket and doesn't take out the funds he needs, it is because he needs to repent and increase his *emunah*. Studying Torah is a blessing but, along with it, one must have a tremendous amount of faith in *Hashem*. This doesn't mean relying on others to bail one out every month, but to be diligent with your time and truly devote yourself to study so that *Hashem* will personally provide for you.

"Anyone who decides to study Torah and not work, making his living from charity, desecrates *Hashem's* name, disgraces the Torah... and any Torah that is not accompanied by work will lead to its own undoing and cause sin..." (Yad Hachazaka, Talmud Torah, 3:10.)

However, in a different statement, Rambam appears to contradict himself. He teaches that the tribe of Levi has a special dispensation from earning a living by its own labor, and he adds:

"And not only the tribe of Levi, but any person whose spirit moves him to separate himself and stand before *Hashem*, to serve Him in order to know Him...behold he has become sanctified as the Holy of Holies, and *Hashem* becomes his portion, his inheritance forever. And He will provide his basic necessities for him in this world, as with the *Kohanim* and *Levi'im*..." (Mishneh Torah, Laws of Shemittah and Yovel 13:13)

The Brisker Rav resolves this apparent contradiction by suggesting that these are the two lifestyles the Talmud teaches:

Rabbi Yishmael emphasizes the verse "And you shall gather your grain." That the study of Torah is to be accompanied by earning a livelihood. Rabbi Shimon bar Yochai, however, contends that "When Israel does the Will of *Hashem*, others will do her work..."The Sage Abaye concludes that "Many did like Rav Yishmael and succeeded; like Rabbi Shimon bar Yochai and did not succeed." (Brachos 35b.)

The Brisker Rav explains that Abaye is saying to choose your own path - but Rabbi Yishmael's is the path for the masses. Rabbi Shimon Bar Yochai's approach works for only a few, determined individuals. The first statement of Maimonides is directed toward the masses. The average person's commitment will not stand up to the demand of full-time Torah. The second statement is relevant to the individual who is able to fulfill such a commitment. (Rabbi Yitzchak Ze'ev Soloveichik the Brisker Rav, Maran R.Y.Z. on the Torah, Parshas Chayei Sarah.)

Rabbi Moshe Isserlis (Rama) quotes Maimonides' first statement, which encourages earning a livelihood. He notes, however, that there are dissenting views and that their opinion is the one that all places in Israel have adopted. (Shulchan Aruch, Laws of Talmud Torah, 246:21)

Rabbi Israel Meir Kagen (Chofetz Chaim) rules that even the Rambam would agree that nowadays one may learn full-time., since it is so difficult for someone to simultaneously devote himself to a livelihood and also master the Torah. (Mishna Brurah, Laws of Brachos 231:1, in the Biur Halacha)

"Rabban Gamliel the son of Rabbi Yehuda the Prince said, good is Torah study together with a worldly occupation, for the exertion in both makes one forget sin. All Torah study without work will result in waste and will cause sinfulness. Anyone who works for the community should work for the sake of Heaven, for the merit of their [the community members'] forefathers will help him, and their righteousness endures forever. And as for you, [says G-d], I will grant you much reward as if you accomplished it on your own." (Pirkey Avos 2:2)

This is a *ben* Torah: (excerpt from A Guide to *Parnasa*)

He knows that any trade - no matter what the conventional wisdom might say about its prospects - can generate prosperity (Mishna, Kiddushin 82a). His *melacha* might be his duty, but it's not the actual source of his success as, in general terms, economic status is decided before birth (Niddah 16b) and the specific details for this year were set last Rosh Hashanah (Beitza 16a - Shabbos, *Yom Tov* and *chinuch* expenses being deductible).

Through self-analysis, he tries to understand how much effort (*hishtadlus*) is appropriate for his unique situation. He realizes that overly intensive involvement in this-worldly pursuits can badly distract him from his Torah life (and cloud his sense of dependence on G-d). On the other hand, he also knows that if he minimizes his effort, relying wholeheartedly on G-d to meet his needs, he might not yet be spiritually ready to face the disappointment of unmet expectations (even if he's intellectually aware that whatever he's been given is no less than G-d intended for him). The trick is finding the proper balance (see R' Dessler, Michtav M'Eliyahu volume 1, page 189).

He enjoys his work and takes pride and satisfaction when he does well. "G-d instills in each man's heart a fondness for his *parnasa*... hence the popular expression: lower a tasty vegetable to a pig and he'll do what he always does (i.e., roll it in the mud as he does with his regular, coarse food — Rashi)." (Brachos 43b) In other words, even a dirty, degrading job can (and should) appear majestic in the eyes of the one doing it (as, according to Rashi "*Yafe lo*", G-d doesn't want any trade to die out). Even more so a job that provides some useful, constructive service to ease the lives of one's fellow human beings.

He looks to his work to provide opportunities for Torah growth: "The majority of camel drivers (who regularly face the dangers of the desert and will thereby turn to G-d as their only hope) are *kosher*; most sailors (who face yet greater dangers at sea) are *Chassidim*." (Kiddushin 82a, see Rashi). In fact, Chovos Halevavos suggests that one of the reasons G-d Himself created His world with the need for people to work was to provide precious opportunities for spiritual challenges and elevation.

He's confident that his self-reliance and hard work are safeguarding his spiritual accomplishments. "Greater than one who fears heaven is one who benefits from his hard work."(Brachos 8a) Maharsha explains that, by earning his own way during his lifetime, a man can ensure that his reward in the next world won't have been prematurely spent miraculously supporting him here.

The Mesilas Yesharim in Chapter 21 writes that, since what's coming to us has already been decreed from Above, we can (when it comes to our material success) simply rely on Him. Why waste any time at all trying to speed things up? Our efforts won't help anyway. In fact, a *ben* Torah will welcome the enjoyment and sense of fulfillment he finds in his work, but he must never forget that the time spent earning a living - though necessary - is time that can be a distraction from the pursuit of his true purpose in creation.

If you take the words וְכָבוֹד עֹשֶׁר wealth and honor -

and add their total, you come to 608. This shares the word בתרו *BesRo*, its half. "A person dies reaching only half of his desires for wealth and honor." (Koheleth Rabbah 1:34) It's never enough, once you have it, you are not satisfied.

If you take just the word עֹשֶׁר which means wealth, it also spells out *Esur*, which is ten, and is also the word *Aser*, which means tithe. A person is supposed to tithe ten percent to charity and *Hashem* will bless him.

"Bring the whole tithe into the storehouse, that there may be food in my house. 'Test me in this,' says the L-rd Almighty, 'and see if I will not throw open the floodgates of heaven and pour out so much blessing that you will not have room enough for it.'" (Malachi 3:10-11)

Using the same letters, we also have the word, שֵׂעָר *SayAR*, which means hair. Just as a person cuts his hair and it grows back even more, so too when a person gives charity, he increases his wealth.

The same letters עֹשֶׁר as also spelled out *bemilu*, equal 1000. "May the L-RD, the G-d of your fathers, make you a thousand times as many as you are and bless you, as He has promised you!" (Deuteronomy 1:11) If a person doesn't use his wealth for *Hashem*, if you flip the letters of עֹשֶׁר you get רשע *rasha*, wicked.

Rashi on the words, בְּזֵעַת אַפֶּיךָ (Genesis 3:19) says: "לאחר שתטריח בו הרבה"– "After you toil a lot." But much toil and you barely put food on the table? לאחר שתטריח – "After you toil," can mean two things: 1) After you are done with thinking that your own toil makes *parnasa*. 2) Reading it with a comma לאחר שתטריח, בו הרבה. After toiling hard by working on your *emunah*, then בו הרבה. This doesn't mean quantity, but rather quality. There will be lots of *shefa*; the money will come from the side of *kedusha*, as opposed to one who thinks he gets money on his own and gets the money from the "other side". A *remez* to this is that בו הרבה is the same *gematria* as טהור.

The Kli Yakar and the *Ohr Hachaim* suggest an answer

based on the Gemara in Brachos (61) that asks why the Torah wrote in the first *parsha* of *Shema* that one must keep this *mitzvah* with his soul and his money. If one must keep it with his soul is it not obvious that he should keep it with all of his money? The Gemara answers that there are some people whose money is more important to them than their lives. Therefore, the Torah wrote that one must keep this *mitzvah* with all his soul and with all his money.

"איזה הוא עשיר השמח בחלקו"

How does one become an עשיר? השמח בחלקו - by being happy with one's lot. Reb Nosson Breslover once told someone with financial troubles that *simcha* is *mesugal* for *parnasa*. The man replied that it was difficult to be happy in his present situation. Reb Nosson responded: "But, what won't a person do for *parnasa*?" (The same story is told over with the Yismach Yisrael of Alexander) Reb Mendel Riminover says a *remez* to *simcha* being *mesugal* for *parnasah* is that the last letters of פותח את ידך and שמח אך והיית are the same and they are a Name connected to *parnasa*.

If you take the entire *posuk* איזה הוא עשיר השמח בחלקו you come to a total of 1080 in the *gematria* method of *AchBi*. This shares the same word as מעשרתיכם *MasRoSayChem*, your tithes. Also, the word מעשר *Mispar Shemi / Milui*. Not only is a person happy because of his lot, but he also becomes happy when he shares and gives from what he has to others.

It says in Kedushin 82b, "It was taught, R. Simeon b. Eleazar said: In my whole lifetime, I have not seen a deer engaged in gathering fruits, a lion carrying burdens, or a fox as a shopkeeper, yet they are sustained without trouble, though they were created only to serve me, whereas I was created to serve my Maker. Now, if these who were created only to serve me are sustained without trouble, how much more should I be sustained without trouble, I who was created to serve my Maker! It is because I have acted evilly and destroyed my livelihood, as it is said, 'your iniquities have turned away these things.'" (Jeremiah 5:25)

It was taught: R. Nehorai said: "I abandon all trades in the world and teach my son only Torah, for every trade in the world stands a man instead only in his youth, and in his old age he is exposed to hunger, but the Torah is not so: it stands by him in his youth and gives him a future and hope in his old age. Of the time of his youth what is said? 'But they that wait upon the L-rd shall renew their strength; they shall mount up with wings as eagles.' (Isaiah 40:31) Of his old age, what is said? 'They shall still bring forth fruit in old age; they shall be full of sap and green.'" (Psalms 92:15) (Kiddushin 82b)

Rashi explains, "The reward for Torah study continues to come to a person throughout his life; even when he is old or sick and can no longer study, he continues to reap the rewards of his previous learning."

"לִי הַכֶּסֶף וְלִי הַזָּהָב נְאֻם יְ-ה-וָ-ה צְבָאוֹת"

"The silver is Mine, and the gold is Mine, says the L-rd of Hosts."(610) (Chaggai 2:8) The only thing within one's power to do to better his economic situation is to entreat *Hashem* with all his heart.

If you use the *gematria* method of *AvGad* you get a total of 610. This also shares the word מעשר *MaaSer*, tithe.

The word בְּרְכַּת blessing comes to a total of ten in the *gematria Mispar Katan* (Reduced). This reminds us that when we give *maaser*, charity and kindness to others, we are also receiving.

Hashem wants nothing more than to shower us with his blessings. Nothing happens above without some action from below. If we repent and do kindness to others, we will remove the obstacles that are hindering our blessing from descending to us. "Your sins have turned away these [blessings] and your transgressions have withheld the good from you." (Jeremiah 5:25)

This is really the difference between us and the other living creatures and organisms of the world who receive their needs without trouble. Their *emunah* in *Hashem* is very simple. They know He will provide rain, bugs, or whatever they need to grow. Daily they praise him as we learn from Perek Shira. The plant, the animal, even the angels haven't been blessed with free will, so they are free from sin. All that is required of them is to know *Hashem's* Oneness with complete faith and they are given their needs.

We too must yearn for *Hashem*, praise Him with simplicity, stay away from sin, and we too will find our daily blessing. When we pray to Him, we must pray with all our bones (עצמתי *AtzMosi*, 610), with all our hearts and being.

As you can see, *Hashem* has an endless amount of treasure He can give us. The entire purpose of Creation was so that He could share with us his goodness. When we realize that everything belongs to Him, even our body and soul begin to merge with Him. Since all Jews are connected, we also give to our fellow when we serve *Hashem* and are upright. We start to realize that if we give of ourselves in kindness to others, we are coming closer to *Hashem* as well. Then the "בִּרְכַּת יְהֹוָה הִיא תַעֲשִׁיר"

The blessing of *Hashem* will bring us riches, because true wealth is knowing *Hashem*. It is the purpose of all the world and the very reason we breathe the breath of life.

Sefer Pesukei Torah

Lesson 16

"וְאָנֹכִי תוֹלַעַת וְלֹא אִישׁ"

"But I am a worm and not a man." (Psalms 22:7)

Dovid HaMelech is clearly pointing out that he has worked hard on becoming humble before *Hashem*. Since he is humble and doesn't think of himself as above his fellow, it is only natural that *Hashem* should now save him and raise him up.

Using the method of *Mispar Siduri*, the *posuk* adds up to a total of 171. This shares the word, הופיע *HofeA* (171), he shined forth. A person who is humble, his soul shines forth. If he was previously dull or unrecognized, he has become polished through humility.

The Talmud teaches, "*Hashem* said to Israel, 'I love you because even when I bestow greatness upon you, you humble yourselves before Me. I bestowed greatness upon Avraham, yet he said to Me, 'I am but dust and ashes' (Genesis 18:27); upon Moshe and Aaron, yet they said to Me, 'We are nothing' (Exodus 16:8); upon Dovid, and he said to Me, 'but I am a worm, and not a man.'" (Chulin 89a) Conversely, when the very fiber of Judaism, the Torah and its commandments are threatened, one must fight like a mighty warrior against all those who try to undermine the word of *Hashem*, as the Talmud teaches, "Be bold as a leopard... to carry out the will of your Father in Heaven." (Avos 5:23)

A person should not say in his heart that he is greater than another or that he serves *Hashem* and is closer to Him than someone else. This is because he, like every other creature, was created to serve *Hashem*. *Hashem* gave to other people understanding just as he gave to him understanding. [Each was given a certain degree of understanding according to what *Hashem* wanted of him.] Why should he consider himself more important than a worm? The worm serves *Hashem* with all its understanding and strength. [We see that] men are also compared to a worm as the verse says, "I am a worm and not a man. "If *Hashem* had not given to him understanding he would not be able to serve Him. He would be like a worm [serving *Hashem* without the understanding of a man.] Since that is the case, he is not more important in heaven then a worm, and certainly not more important than any other man. He should consider himself on the level of a worm, and that all other small creatures are his friends in this world. All of them were created [by *Hashem*], and they do not have any power by themselves [without Him.] They can only do what *Hashem* has given them the strength and understanding to do. This should always be in your thoughts. (P. 414, Sefer Baal Shem Tov, teachings of the Baal Shem Tov.)

"Fear not, O' worm of Jacob, *(tolaas Yaacov)*." (Isaiah 41:14) The Jewish people is called "the worm of Yacov" for, although they are as weak as a worm, their power is in their mouth - the power of prayer (a worm can bring down a giant cedar tree with its mouth and so can the Jewish People bring down its giant enemies with prayer).

Is Isaiah using the term worm simply as a bleak description of the state of the people, or is something else being implied by this description?

Rashi on this verse suggests that the Jewish people may have been as weak as worms, but "*She'ain lakh gevurah ela ba'peh.* [Their strength was in their mouths.]" The mouth is good for at least two things, one of which, prayer, is the most powerful.

The worm then becomes a spiritual metaphor for spiritual and prayerful strength. The worm perseveres. It crawls forward very slowly and yet, despite all the hazards in its way, it finally arrives at its destination. "Who gives the tired strength, and to him who has no strength, He increases strength. Now youths shall become tired and weary, and young men shall stumble, but those who put their hope in the Lord shall renew [their] vigor, they shall raise wings as eagles; they shall run and not weary, they shall walk and not tire." (Isaiah 40:29-31)

Interestingly, using the *gematria* style of *Ofanim*, the original *posuk* adds up to the total 516, which shares the word, אשירה *ashira*, I will sing. It is the song of prayer that will now break through and help a person to overcome his enemies. Song leads to rejoicing, which really is the goal of humility: to rejoice over the simple understanding that *Hashem* is King over all the earth.

With the method of *Mispar Ne'elam* (with the *posuk*), we get a total of 754. This joins with the word, ושמחת *VSaMachta*, you shall rejoice. People who have pride always have to pretend to be happy while someone who thinks of himself as lowly, not speaking about brokenheartedness but true humility; he feels a true rejoicing and satisfaction in life at its root.

A person is נסוס *NaSos*, tested in life in order to prove himself. He usually finds that the only way to pass the obstacles placed before him is to humble himself. Using the *gematria* style of *Ofanim*, נסוס (516), tested, comes out to the same value as the *posuk* which Dovid HaMelech cried out: that I am a worm and not a man. I have reached the level of absolute humility; therefore, the test must be concluded, and salvation must come.

Therefore, using the method of *AvGad* (with the *posuk*) (719), we come to the word והשבותו *VaHaShaVoSo*, you have restored and returned it. A person will find in life that, should he take the 'high road' and not argue or be overly proud, then his bounty and blessing will be restored to him.

Someone asked the Maggid of Mezeritch, "In as much as it is written, 'Truth springs forth from the ground', truth should certainly be available in great abundance. Why is it that falsehood seems to prevail, and truth is such a rarity?"

The *maggid* answered, "It is because when truth springs forth from the ground, it remains at a low height, and in order to pick it up one must stoop down. But no one wishes to humble himself to pick up the truth."

Truth is G-dliness, and if one is aware of the infinity of his duties toward *Hashem*, he cannot but be humble. One of the Chassidic masters said, "I am so grateful that *ga'avah* (vanity) is not a *mitzvah*. If it were, what could I possibly be vain about?"

The Rabbi of Kotzk, referring to the above verse that "Truth springs forth from the ground," said that growth from the ground first requires planting. "If you bury falsehood, truth will grow." (Smiling Each Day, p. 324)

So, this is the greatness of the worm, and in fact of the Jewish people. We are the greatest nation of the world, yet we are humble about it. If we need something, we lower ourselves and pray to *Hashem* for help. We live our lives slowly, thinking before we do any action. We remain a small nation, yet our impact on society has no equal. You cannot compare us to other societies who are just simple men; nobody has been through the trials that we have faced throughout history. We have been the dust that people trample upon, yet from our mouths are words of song and praise.

There was once a ruler who wasn't able to have children. He went to his advisers and they suggested that he "force" the Jews to pray for him, as throughout generations their G-d always listen to their cries. So, he made a decree that if he didn't have a child they would all be put to death. It wasn't long before the Jewish community prayed heartfelt prayers to *Hashem* for salvation and the ruler had a son.

When we, the Jewish people, are humbled like a worm, we realize our special gifts as Jews. It is at that time that we reconnect ourselves to our Master in heaven. So why wait till the last moment? Let us humble ourselves now and be subservient to *Hashem*.

Lesson 17

"לֹא יָשַׁבְתִּי עִם מְתֵי שָׁוְא וְעִם נַעֲלָמִים
לֹא אָבוֹא"

"I did not sit with dishonest men, neither did I go with hypocrites."(Psalms 26:4)

People underestimate how influenced they are by their surroundings. For one reason or another, they make excuses to hang around negative people. Whether it's because of business, family, peer pressure, honor, or what have you, they find themselves in situations that have no benefit for their souls. It could even be a matter of preferring not to make changes in their lives.

The *Mispar Siduri* of this *posuk* totals 349, which shares the word, השמיד *HashMaid*, destroy. If you don't learn to separate yourself from negative influences, they will one day take over your thoughts and destroy you from the outside in.

Many are even in denial about their friendships, thinking for years that their comrades care about them and would stand by their side through thick and thin. Little do they know that the person is using them for alternative reasons.

"לֹא יָשַׁבְתִּי עִם מְתֵי שָׁוְא" If you take just the words,

You come to a total sum in *Mispar Siduri* of 191, which is the word ונקלה *ViNeakLa*, and be dishonored. While all the time you think they are your friends and protection, they are really dishonoring you because they don't respect who you really are. Life is just a game to them, like a game of chess, trying to overpower people to follow in their footsteps.

The Psalmist is telling us, I didn't get to where I am today by being around dishonest people who curse, talk negatively or waste away their days. I am here where I am because I was willing to separate myself from bad people and hypocrites.

Not only this, but I also surrounded myself with holy

people and people who want to draw close to You. This gave me the emotional support I needed to better myself and strive for perfection.

"לֹא יָשַׁבְתִּי עִם מְתֵי שָׁוְא"

If you take just the words, using the *gematria* style of *Ofanim*, you have the word תחתיו *TachTav* (824), under him; because the place to become holy is under the feet of the sages, as it says in Pirkey Avos (1:4): "Yose ben Yoezer of Tzereidah and Yose ben Yochanan of Jerusalem received the tradition from them. Yose ben Yoezer of Tzereidah said, "Let your house be a meeting place for the wise; sit in the dust at their feet, and drink in their words thirstily."

If we don't have access to the sages because of where we live or our lack of boldness to stand up and draw ourselves close, then it also helps to hear stories of the sages.

Rebbe Nachman once remarked, "What most inspired me to devote myself to serving G-d in truth was hearing stories about *tzaddikim*." He explained that many great *tzaddikim* used to visit his parents' house, which had once been the home of the Baal Shem Tov (Rebbe Nachman's maternal great-grandfather). These illustrious chassidim would come frequently to Medzeboz to pray at the Baal Shem Tov's grave, and on their way most of them would visit Rebbe Nachman's parents.

Thus, during his youth, the *rebbe* came to hear their stories, which awakened in his soul the burning desire to serve G-d and to strive for the highest spiritual levels (Rabbi Nachman's Wisdom #138).

Lesson 18

"אַחַת שָׁאַלְתִּי מֵאֵת יְ-ה-וָ-ה אוֹתָה
אֲבַקֵּשׁ שִׁבְתִּי בְּבֵית יְ-ה-וָ-ה כָּל יְמֵי חַיַּי
לַחֲזוֹת בְּנֹעַם

יְ-ה-וָ-ה וּלְבַקֵּר בְּהֵיכָלוֹ"

*"One [thing] I ask of the L-rd, that I seek -
that I may dwell in the house of the L-rd all the
days of my life, to see the pleasantness of the L-rd
and to visit His Temple every morning."(Psalms
27:4)*

    If you take the *Mispar Siduri* value of the entire *posuk,*
you get a total of 683, which matches the word, והעברת
VhaaVarTa, you shall separate and set apart. You have a choice:
do you wish to seek *Hashem* with your complete spirit, or do
you wish to serve Him half-heartedly? To dwell in the house
of *Hashem,* to make yourself into a walking Temple for *Hashem,*
you must be willing to separate from others.

    People soak up your time that could otherwise be used
for learning; they drain your very being with their materialistic
yearnings and take you away from *Hashem* along with them.

"לַחֲזוֹת בְּנֹעַם יְ-ה-וָ-ה"

"To see the pleasantness of the Lord."

    Using the *gematria* type of *Mispar Siduri* on just these
words, you get a total of 137, which shares the word בפיהם
BiFeeHem, in their mouths. Where do you see the pleasantness
of *Hashem?* In the mouths of the *tzaddikim* whose words are
attached to the *Shechinah.* The sage speaks with *sechal,* sweetness
and fear of *Hashem.* By being close to the sages, you draw from
this light and experience a glimpse of the sweetness of *Hashem.*

Another way to experience the sweetness is to spread His Oneness. *VHoDaTa*, and you shall make known to them the path in which they should go and the deeds that they should do (Shemos 18:20). וְהוֹדַעְתָּ *VHoDaTa*, and you shall make known, is *gematria* Reverse *AvGad* of 491, which is the same value as these words לַחֲזוֹת בְּנֹעַם יְ-ה-וָ-ה. Therefore, you can see that, to taste the sweetness of *Hashem*, you should teach the ways of *Hashem*. When you spread the Torah to others, *Hashem* opens the Torah's hidden meanings to you.

One of the ways to appreciate *Hashem's* sweetness is to look at the beauty in our children. They are a reflection of His beauty and purity. Using *gematria AvGad* on the words לַחֲזוֹת בְּנֹעַם יְ-ה-וָ-ה, you also get a total of 297 which shares the word, זַרְעֲךָ *zarAcha*, your seed. In your life you might find yourself in dark places or confusion, but when you look at your offspring and your blessings, then you should feel the pleasantness of *Hashem*.

Also sharing the *AvGad* total is the word, אַרְצוֹ *ArtZo*, his land. If you appreciate the land of *Eretz Yisrael* and its holiness, you also feel the pleasantness of *Hashem*. To do this, you must become a part of its holiness through dwelling in the land or giving charity to the poor or *yeshivos* in *Eretz Hakodesh*-because עֶזְרָךָ *EzRaCha*, your help, is the same total as אַרְצוֹ *Artzo*, his land.

"בְּבֵית יְ-ה-וָ-ה"

We know that this is referring to the holy Temple and the houses of prayer and study. However, it also is referring to one's own place, as we see from the *AvGad gematria* value of בְּבֵית יְ-ה-וָ-ה sixty-six being equivalent to the word, אֹהָלֶיךָ *OHaLecha*, your tents. You can bring the *Shechinah* anywhere if you seek *Hashem*, and hence you should make your home a place for the *Shechinah* to rest. People sometimes live two types of lifestyles, one which they share with their community and the other behind closed doors. We see from this *gematria* that it is just as important if not more so to make your home a sanctuary for holiness.

If you add one to אהליך *OHaLecha*, your tents, you have the word ואמך *VEimCha*, and your mother. You can tell a lot about a person by how he treats his mother. If a person can't treat his mother with sweetness, he certainly won't know how to make a

"בְּבֵית יְ-הֹ-וָ-ה "

Which is a dwelling house for the *Shechinah*, but what about one's mother-in-law? Using the *gematria* style of *Mispar Ne'elam*, חתנתו (mother-in-law) totals 864 as does בְּבֵית יְ-הֹ-וָ-ה. It is also important to show her honor and respect.

"וּלְבַקֵּר בְּהֵיכָלוֹ"

"and to visit His Temple every morning"

Every morning we are given our soul to serve *Hashem* with a new beginning, to start completely anew like a child at birth, and renew our covenant with Him. These words,

"וּלְבַקֵּר בְּהֵיכָלוֹ "

equal the value in *Mispar Siduri* of 105 which is the word, להמל *LiHeMoal*, to be circumcised. We must grab the new opportunity we are given every morning and not take it for granted. How we start our day is how we most likely will finish it. "Arise like a lion to serve your Creator in the morning." (Shulchan Aruch 1,1)

Sefer Pesukei Torah

Lesson 19

"קוֹל יְ-ה-וָ-ה חֹצֵב לַהֲבוֹת אֵשׁ"

"The voice of the L-rd cleaves with flames of fire." (Psalms 29:7)

Rashi says on this *posuk*, "Our Sages (*Mechilta* ibid.) explained that the utterance of the Decalogue emanated from His mouth with a flame of fire and was engraved on the tablets according to their form."

If you take just the words,

"לַהֲבוֹת אֵשׁ"

It is the numerical value of sixty-nine in *gematria Mispar Siduri* which shares the word, הסובב *HaSovaiv*, to surround. The flames of fire surround the letters of the Torah.

We learn from *Chazal* that the Torah was given with its writing on fire. The white fire means *Chochmah*, the second *Sefirah*. This is the white substratum upon which the black letters are written. The black letters (black fire) mean *Binah*. The white fire is the written Torah and the black fire is the oral Torah. The image of black fire over white fire conveys the interrelation of the oral and written Torahs. What we have today and consider the written Torah is not exactly the same as the written Torah of white fire. The Torah we read, of black ink handwritten on parchment, is perceived through the prism of the oral Torah of black fire. Only someone who has attained the level of prophecy can still perceive the written Torah of white fire. (Taken from my *sefer* Chassidus, Kabbalah and Meditation)

If you take the entire *posuk* "קוֹל יְ-ה-וָ-ה חֹצֵב לַהֲבוֹת אֵשׁ" you get a total *gematria* value of 1006. This shares the word תורת *Toras*. "And it shall be for you a sign on your arm and a reminder between your eyes - so that *Hashem*'s Torah may be in your mouth." (Psalms 29:7)

The voice of the L-rd cleaves with flames of fire.

The voice of *Hashem* is the Torah. It is His voice to us, teaching us how to live our lives, but it is not just the written Torah that is important. The oral Torah that is perceived in His *Kol*; therefore, it is also seen in flames. The word, ושש *VShaShes*, and six, also totals 1006. It is the six orders of the *Mishnah* that, if you reverse their letters, you have the word *neshamah*. It is the study of the *Mishnah* that is sometimes neglected, as a person tries to study other books that are easier to understand. Yet it is the study of *Mishnah* that has a direct correlation to one's soul.

You look with your eyes and see the holy letters of the Hebrew alphabet, and then you perceive the face of *Hashem*. If you take the *posuk*, "קוֹל יְ-ה-וָ-ה חֹצֵב לַהֲבוֹת אֵשׁ" in *Mispar Siduri* you get a total of 160, which shares the words עֵינֶיךָ *AiyNecha*, your eyes; פָּנֶיךָ *Panecha*, your face; עָיֵף *AaYaif*, faint; and נֹפֵל *Nofail*, to fall down. These three words are exactly what happened at the receiving of the Torah. What happened during the giving of the Torah? The Jews saw thunder. The moment of the giving of our Torah, *zman matan toraseinu*, was an extraordinary event. "All the people saw the thunder and the lightning, the blare of the horn and the mountain smoking; and when the people saw it, they fell back and stood at a distance." (Exodus 20:15) It was so miraculous that the people saw what normally could only be heard. They saw thunder!

So, if your desire is to come close to *Hashem* and fear Him, cling to the holy letters and the Torah. That is where the *Shechinah* can be found.

The Torah offers many faces and speaks with even more voices. The tradition also teaches that there are seventy faces of the Torah, *shivim panim laTorah*. This is often explained to mean that there are seventy different ways of reading our most sacred text, but you can also understand it to mean that there are seventy different pathways.

"ת"ר הרואה אוכלוסי ישראל אומר ברוך חכם הרזים שאין דעתם דומה זה לזה ואין פרצופיהן דומים זה לזה"

The *rabbis* have taught: "He who sees crowds of

Israelites should say, 'Blessed... Who is wise in secrets' because their minds differ, and their faces differ." (Berachos 58a)

Even though *Chazal* teach us this, we still have no limitations on hurting our fellow Jews through our close-mindedness. If another Jew doesn't share our same *rebbe, rav,* or beliefs we shouldn't look at him as if something is wrong with him.

Nothing in this world looks, feels, or sounds exactly like another creature. This too, is reminding us that *Hashem* likes us each to serve Him in unique ways (of course, according to *halacha*).

The school of R. Ishmael taught, "As a hammer shatters a rock." (Jeremiah 23:29) Just as a hammer subdivides a rock into many different sparks, so does the biblical verse extend into many different interpretations (Sanhedrin 34a).

Hence the code word for biblical commentary, which encompasses different approaches to the same verse, is *PaRDeS* (literally meaning orchard), comprising *P'shat* (the plain meaning of the text), *Remez* (symbolic meaning of the text), *D'rash* (rabbinical explication of the text), and *Sod* (the secret, mystical meaning of the text). The sum total of these add up to the "seventy faces" of the Torah, symbolizing the seventy nations of the world, the seventy distinctive approaches to life, reflecting the myriad possibilities and entranceways to the meaning of the Bible and to an understanding (however imperfect and incomplete) of the Divine.

Just as a gem's facets all contribute to its magnificence, as every way you turn the diamond you see a different angle of light shining from it, so too the different types of *perush* are not contradictory but rather complementary. It could also be understood when compared to a symphony - there are multiple instruments playing in harmony.

The voice of the L-rd cleaves with flames of fire. (Psalms 29:7)

Not only are there many ways to understand the Torah, but each person's revelation on *Har Sinai* was also different.

None of us feel the exact same emotions and even our eyes may see colors differently than our fellow. But yet, we are so quick to judge.

Lesson 20

"וְאָהַבְתָּ לְרֵעֲךָ כָּמוֹךָ אֲנִי יְ-ה-וָ-ה"

"You shall love your neighbor as yourself. I am the L-rd." (Psalms 19:18)

Rashi says, "You shall love your neighbor as yourself." Rabbi Akiva says, "This is a fundamental [all-inclusive] principle of the Torah." (Toras Kohanim 19:45)

Why is it that the *posuk* adds the words, 'I am *Hashem*' at the end? It is because, if a person loves his fellow with all his heart, then he finds *Hashem*. Should a person not know how to love another, how could he love *Hashem*? Therefore, if you don't fulfill this *posuk*, and you don't properly love your neighbor, you don't have *Hashem* in your life. *Ani Hashem* is also a reminder that, "we cannot be more righteous than *Hashem*." (Bamidbar Rabbah 12:2) As in this aspect nobody's love, your neighbor's or anyone's, is like *Hashem's* unconditional love. Yet we must learn from His example and try because this is the foundation of the world.

There is a story about a gentile who came before Shammai and said to him, "I will convert if you teach me the entire Torah while I stand on one foot." Shammai pushed him away with the measuring stick that was in his hand. The gentile then went to Hillel, who helped him to convert. Hillel told him, "Whatever is hateful to you do not do to your friend. This is the entire Torah. The rest is its explanation. Go and study."

Reb Dovid of Lelov understood this principle at a young age. As a young man living in his father-in-law's house, he practiced a severe regimen of self-affliction. His father-in-law, a simple man, could not understand such strange behavior. When he heard how Reb Dovid would immerse himself in frozen lakes, or roll naked in the snow as penance, he became enraged. Once he even threw Reb Dovid out of the house, and one of the servants had to let him in through a back door. Yet the servant was also bewildered by Reb Dovid's actions. "Have you really sinned so much that you must afflict yourself so?" he asked. "What can I do?" replied Reb Dovid. "I still have not reached the level of complete love for all Jews."

Reb Dovid of Lelov used to say, "Every Jew has a core of complete goodness, even if he himself is unaware of it. The bad is only external, not intrinsic to his soul at all. "The inner Jewish soul is simply not inclined to sin.

"It is impossible to find bad in a Jew," said the Chidushei haRim, in Reb Dovid's name.

If you take the words,

וְאָהַבְתָּ לְרֵעֲךָ כָּמוֹךָ אֲנִי יְ-ה-וָ-ה

You come to a total of 211 in *gematria Mispar Siduri*. This shares the word, וגר *VvGair*, and the convert. We are commanded to love the convert equivalently as we would someone born as a Jew.

In *gematria* style *AvGad* of the entire *posuk*, you get a total of 707, which shares the word, אשתו *EishTo*, his wife. *Hashem* gave a person a partner that he should love completely as himself. Many couples go through their marriage thinking they are still two entities, but when they don't provide for their spouse's needs they only hurt themselves. Therefore, when we treat our partner as ourselves, then we also have Hashem in our lives.

The convert, the wife and the neighbor all give us the opportunity to learn to love outside ourselves and, through this, to find *Hashem*.

If you take just the words,

וְאָהַבְתָּ לְרֵעֲךָ כָּמוֹךָ

You get a sum of 160 in *Mispar Siduri*, which equals the *posuk* from the last lesson also in *Mispar Siduri* 160,

"קוֹל יְ-ה-וָ-ה חֹצֵב לַהֲבוֹת אֵשׁ"

"The voice of the Lord cleaves with flames of fire." (Psalms 29:7)

Which we connected to the giving of the Torah, the holiness of its letters and (metaphorically) seeing the Face of *Hashem*. Through loving one's fellow, the fire of Torah becomes open to a person. That is why it's so important to teach Torah to others.

What is a true friend? Someone who cares enough about your *neshamah* to tell you words of Torah and *d'vekus*. If he doesn't take an interest in your spiritual well-being, he isn't a real friend.

Our Sages state: "One should not take leave of his friend except amidst words of *halacha.*" According to our holy *rebbeim*, this alludes to the kind of Torah teaching that propels the listener and transforms him into a *mehalech* - one who ascends from level to level, and from peak to peak... (*HaYOM YOM 6 Iyar*)

Rabbi Akiva said: "For man was created in the image of God," meaning that, even if a person is not particular about his own honor, he should be particular about the honor of his friend.

If you take just the words,

Love your fellow וְאָהַבְתָּ לְרֵעֶךָ

You get a sum in *Mispar Siduri* of 107, which is the word לנגדך *LiNegDecha*, equally with you.

Reb Dovid of Lelov supported himself with a small grocery store. Once a customer entered the shop and asked him where he could buy salt. Reb Dovid first listed all the other stores in town, and only then concluded, "And you can buy it here if you like." Another morning, when he arrived at work, he noticed that his competitor's store was still closed. He ran to wake him. "Get up quickly!" he urged. "Customers are already coming!"

In *AvGad gematria*, you reach a total of 469 with the words

וְאָהַבְתָּ לְרֵעֶךָ

You also have the same word as והאזנת *VHaAZanTa*, and you shall give ear. The main thing about being a good friend or spouse is to just listen.

A person needs to love; it is human nature too. "Two of each shall you bring into the *Ark 'LiHaChayos*, to keep alive with you'". In the *gematria* style of *Mispar Bone'eh*, *LiHachayos*

לההית (453) is the same numerical value as, וְאָהַבְתָּ (453), and love.

Because we all need love in our life to keep us breathing. ·

Whether it is love for *Hashem*, others, or even the love we have to accomplish our hopes and dreams. Without this, we don't feel alive.

The problem is that sometimes when we don't have the right love in our life or we don't know how to love, we start to cling to and love the wrong things.

If you take the word

וְאָהַבְתָּ

And love,

The *gematria* equals 414, which shares the words יְקְדֹשׁ *YekDosh*, shall be holy, and הַקְדֵישָׁה *HakDayshaa*, the harlot. One should be careful and use love in order to be holy and closer to *HaShem*.

So how do you do make sure that your love is pure? Well in the *gematria* style of *AchBi*,

וְאָהַבְתָּ (73) = מלג *MeLog*, to measure (73).

Love must be balanced and calculated, not just be given without limits or balance. That is why in the *Sefiros*, *Hashem* has both *Chesed* and *Gevurah* with *Tiferes* in the middle to balance them. So, love must go along with חכמה *Chochmah (73)*, which is also the value of וְאָהַבְתָּ.

In *AvGad gematria* we see the equivalent value as the word אחי *Achi* (19), my brother. So *mamash*, you know we are all brothers and sisters. We must love each other as such and this will bring us to the final redemption.

Rabbi Shneur Zalman of Liadi said, A person who recognizes the loftiness of the soul, as contrasted to the lowliness of the body, can easily fulfill the *mitzvah* of loving one's fellow. All Jews are interconnected, and all are children of One Father, and therefore we are called brothers, since each person's soul has its root within G-d, and one is only divided from the other in the physical sense. On the other hand, one who gives precedence to the physical will not be able to truly fulfill this *mitzvah* in an unconditional way, as required. That is why Hillel described this *mitzvah* as the most fundamental commandment in the Torah, while the rest is commentary. For the foundation of the service of G-d is to elevate one's soul to its root and thereby draw down spiritual sustenance for the Jewish people, which is not possible to do if we are divided. (Tanya chapter 32)

Lesson 21

"חִזְקוּ וְיַאֲמֵץ לְבַבְכֶם כָּל הַמְיַחֲלִים

לַ יְ-ה-וָ-ה"

*"Strengthen yourselves, and He will give
your heart courage, all who hope to the L-rd."
(Psalms 31:25)*

Rashi explains the simple meaning of the *posuk* to be, "As you see that He did for me, to save me because I hoped for Him." It is hope in *Hashem* that gives a person strength and courage. The moment a person loses hope, he has nothing to hold onto; his courage is lost. Strengthen yourself in *emunah* and hope, because this is everything.

If you take the *gematria* for the entire *posuk*, you get a total of 611 which is equivalent to יראת *Yiras*, fear of *Hashem*. When you fear *Hashem*, you will be strengthened.

Most importantly, to strengthen yourself you must learn more Torah. Numerically equivalent to the *posuk* is the word, תורה *Torah*, also equal to 611.

How else can a person strengthen himself? Through הברית *HaBris* (617), the covenant; this is also numerically equivalent to the *posuk* in *Mispar Kolel*.

When G-d told Avraham to circumcise himself, He said: "And you shall guard my *bris* (covenant), you and your descendants after you for all their generations." (Bereishis 17:9)

This covenant of the *bris milah* is the most important reminder we have that we are holy and chosen by *Hashem*. When a person is pure, his bond with *Hashem* increases and blessing flows through the entire world. They are strengthened and enlightened.

When a person guards the holy covenant, it is as if he had observed the entire Torah, because the Covenant is equal to the whole Torah. (Zohar 197a)

"When a person guards the covenant, which is *Hashem's* seal, death departs from him." (Tikkuney Zohar *97*, Tikkun 22) Being pure also will guard you and give you life. That means an increase in *parnasa*, health, peace, and tranquility.

Through keeping the holy covenant, we know Him, but we can't know Him in sadness. I mean, He is with us regardless if we are up or down. "If I would ascend to heaven, You are there; and if I were to make my bed in the grave, You are there." (Psalms 139:8) But to truly know Him and be close, to keep the Covenant properly, one needs joy in his heart. As it says, "Rejoice, you righteous, in *Hashem*." (Psalms 97:12)

"הַמְיַחֲלִים לַ יְ-ה-וָ-ה"

Hope in *Hashem* is equivalent to צְדָקָה *Tzedaka*, righteousness. If all you have is hope in *Hashem*, this is enough to lead you on the righteous path. Don't live another day without dreaming, believing in *Hashem*, miracles, and hope. If not, you are living in וְעֲלָטָה *VaAlata*, thick darkness, which shares the same *gematria* 120 as הַמְיַחֲלִים לַ יְ-ה-וָ-ה in Mispar Siduri.

"And the earth was desolate and void - *veHaaretz Hayta Tohu vaBohu*." (Genesis 1:2)

"*Vayehi Or* And there will be light." Light always follows darkness. You just have to push through the darkness and the light is there waiting. In that light is *Hashem*. "And *Hashem* saw that light, that it was good. *Ki Tov;* that it was good. The Zohar explains that the light was thrown everywhere - above, below, and on all sides. This was by virtue of the name YKVK, the name which embraces all sides. The Zohar continues and says the Central Pillar (of the *Sefiros*) was complete in itself and made peace on all sides; additional light was lent to it from above and from all sides through the universal joy in it. (Zohar 16b)

You see, the world is simply filled with light. You just have to plug yourself in.

"Rabbi Pinchas of Koretz entered the house of study, and his disciples fell into a profound silence. He asked: 'What were you talking about just now?'

'We were saying how afraid we were that the *Yetzer hara*, evil inclination, will pursue us.'

'Don't worry,' said he. 'You haven't reached that point yet. Right now, you are still pursuing it!'"

Most of the darkness and emptiness a person feels in his life is self-created. People lose hope too easily and forget to be dreamers. "When the L-rd returns the returnees to Zion, we shall be like dreamers." (Psalms 126:1)

"בְּשׁוּב יְ-ה-וָ-ה אֶת שִׁיבַת צִיּוֹן הָיִינוּ כְּחֹלְמִים"

The L-rd returns the returnees to Zion, we shall be like dreamers, is the same *gematria* in *Mispar Siduri* as חדשה *ChAdasha* (317), new. When a person looks at each day as a new opportunity to serve *Hashem*, to dream and accomplish, then *Hashem* returns to Zion. Then He turns "sadness and sighing," (Isaiah 35:10) into joy. As the next *posuk* says,

"אָז יִמָּלֵא שְׂחוֹק פִּינוּ וּלְשׁוֹנֵנוּ רִנָּה"

"Then our mouth will be filled with laughter and our tongue with song." (Psalms 126:2) Rabbi Hirsch explains this *posuk* to mean, "We will explode with happy laughter at the unexpected miraculous turn of events."

So, let us review the order of events that need to take place. First, we must have faith in *Hashem* and dream. This will bring us to happiness because through faith and dreaming of the future, we experience change, miracles.

All Ezekiel needed to do was get through the thick clouds and beyond that was his revelation. So too, with us. We must hold onto our *emunah* and hope when we do, that salvation and light will soon come. May it be His will, Amen.

Let us say no to darkness and negative thoughts that mislead us. Let positivity reign and be foremost. Then,

"וְיַאֲמֵץ לְבַבְכֶם"

He will give us courage that will not let this world trip us into sadness, anxiety, and hopelessness, but rather one that will lead us to Zion, redemption.

"בֹּא יָבֹא בְרִנָּה נֹשֵׂא אֲלֻמֹּתָיו"

"Return in exultation, a bearer of his sheaves."
So, let us remind ourselves,

"חִזְקוּ וְיַאֲמֵץ לְבַבְכֶם כָּל הַמְיַחֲלִים לַיְ-ה-וָ-ה'"

"Strengthen yourselves, and He will give your heart courage, all who hope to the L-rd."

Lesson 22

"לֹא בַשָּׁמַיִם, הוּא"

"It is not in Heaven."(Deuteronomy 30:12)

The *gematria Kollel* of these words equals תגלה *SGaleh* (438), you shall uncover.

The phrase, "Not in Heaven", is understood to justify man's authority to interpret the Torah. The Talmud explains, "[The Torah] is not in Heaven", to mean that the meaning of the *Torah* itself is to be uncovered by man's interpretation and decision-making. (Baba Metzia 59b)

In the academic study of Jewish law, the verse "Not in Heaven" serves as the Biblical grounding for the jurisprudential structure of *halacha* (Jewish law). The source for rabbinic authority is really from Deuteronomy 17:11 (According to the law which they shall teach you, and according to the judgment which they shall tell you, you shall do). As one author explains, thanks to the Midrashic reading of the verse, "...G-d himself acquiesced in His exclusion from the *halachic* process. Having revealed His will at Sinai in the groundwork, He Himself, according to the rabbinic explanation, entrusted the interpretation of His will to the sages."

Even though the Torah is not in Heaven, its wisdom is still difficult to uncover for mankind. Even Moshe Rabbenu had to be retaught the Torah countless times while he up on the mountain. בכיתו *BKiSo* (438), his weeping and praying to *Hashem* to open up his mind to its mysteries, was necessary. Finally, *Hashem* gave it to him as a gift, yet the fiftieth gate was still closed.

If the Torah isn't in *Shamayim*, why should one have to toil not only in hard work to understand it but also in prayer to *Hashem* to reveal its mysteries?

It is because *Hashem* wants a person to prevail over

Him, to defeat Him in a sense. Let's go to a story in the Talmud that shows *Hashem's* appreciation for the hard work of *Torah* students.

There was once a dispute between Rabbi Eliezer ben Hyrcanus and the sages. Rabbi Eliezer brought every possible argument and went to prove it by changing nature. The sages replied each time that you can't do that to prove your point. Eventually, even a *Bas Kol* was heard from Heaven confirming Rabbi Eliezer's opinion in which *Rav* Joshua remarked,

"לֹא בַשָּׁמַיִם, הִוא"

It is not in Heaven.

Following the dispute, Rav Natan met Eliyahu and asked him: "What did *Hashem*, blessed be He, do in that hour?" Eliyahu responded and said "ואמר חייך קא בני נצחוני בני נצחוני

-*KA CHAYICH V'AMAR "NITZCHUNI BANAI, NITZCHUNI BANAI"*

"He was laughing and saying, 'My children have prevailed over Me, My children have prevailed over Me.'"

Rebbe Nachman teaches, "When a person speaks to *Hashem* and uses every kind of argument and appeal to 'conquer' *Hashem*, then *Hashem* Himself has great joy and pleasure from this. He will send words to this person's mouth so that he will be able to 'conquer' Him. How else could flesh and blood win a victory against *Hashem*? It is only because *Hashem* Himself helps us." (Likutei Aitzos, *hisbodedus*)

If you take the words, "My children have prevailed over Me, My children have prevailed over Me."

בני נצחוני בני נצחוני

You come to a total *gematria Reverse AvGad* of 462. This shares the word ואתנה *VETayNa*, and I will give. Through prayer and hard work, *Hashem* will give you mastery of the Torah.

Let's just take בני נצחוני one time and we see another revelation in the *gematria Atbash* which totals 552. How else do you overcome all obstacles, by ושמרו *VShamru*, and you shall keep, מצותיו *Mitzvos*av, his commandments. Both share the *gematria* of the *posuk*, 552. You prevail by keeping the *mitzvos* and the Torah. This allows you to overcome *Hashem*, so to speak.

How else can you defeat *Hashem*? Well, when a decree is against a person in Heaven, sometimes the only way to overturn it is to give charity. As it says, "Charity saves a person from death." Charity can also defeat any obstacle and change the natural order of events. Therefore, the same *gematria Mispar Musafi* of בני נצחוני בני נצחוני

Is equivalent to עשר *AaSair*, to tithe one's money (570).

In the Eruvin 55a, Avdimi bar Ḥama bar Dosa said: What is the meaning of that which is written: "It is not in heaven...nor is it beyond the sea."? (Deuteronomy 30:12-13) "It is not in heaven" indicates that if it were in heaven, you would have to ascend after it, and if it were beyond the sea, you would have to cross after it. Rashi explains that one must expend whatever effort is necessary in order to study Torah.

Expounding the verse differently, Rava said, "It is not in heaven" means that Torah is not to be found in someone who raises his mind over it, like the heavens. The Maharsha explains he thinks his mind is above the Torah and he does not need a teacher; nor is it to be found in someone who expands his mind over it, like the sea. The Maharsha explains that he thinks he knows everything there is to know about the topic he has studied and doesn't feel he must review it. So too, he is not careful not to forget it.

Rabbi Yochanan said: "It is not in heaven," means that Torah is not to be found in the haughty, those who raise their self-image as though they were in heaven. "Nor is it beyond the sea," means that it is not to be found among merchants or traders who are constantly traveling and do not have the time to study Torah properly. Rashi further explains that a Torah scholar must spend most of his time studying indoors and not be out in the streets pursuing his affairs.

The Gemara (Niddah 70b) states that the people of Alexandria, Egypt, asked Rabbi Yehoshua ben Chananya: "What should a person do in order to become wise [in

Torah]?"He answered, "Spend more time in studying and less in business." Rav 'Shas' Cohen explains this Gemara to mean that Rabbi Yehoshua ben Chananyah did not retract his original counsel but added to it another essential condition. To merit the Torah's wisdom, it is not enough to be very diligent in studying and to minimize other pursuits, but one must also pray to the Holy One, blessed be He, beseeching Him to bestow wisdom and knowledge of Torah.

Now that you know that the Torah is not in Heaven, that doesn't mean you should look at it any less. The Torah is still heavenly. The more you purify yourself and work to become a vessel to house the Torah here on earth, the greater your revelation of it, will be.

The Talmud warns us how difficult it is to keep the Torah within you. As it says, "The words of Torah are as difficult to acquire as golden vessels [which are very expensive] and as easy to lose as glass ones [which are very fragile]."(Chagigah 15a)

Anyone can study the Torah; it is there for the taking. However, to acquire the Torah, one must have purity. Besides purity, the Torah must come first.

The Gemara says in Brachos 35b: "Rabbah bar *Channah* said in the name of Rabbi Yochanan [who said it] in the name of Rabbi Yehudah bar Rabbi Ila'i: 'Come and see how the previous generations were unlike these generations. The earlier generations used to make Torah their constant occupation, and business their occasional occupation. They were successful in both. The later generations, who made business their constant occupation and Torah their occasional occupation, were successful in neither.'"

Therefore, we must prioritize our lives and put forward that which is most important. We must make deep reflections on our true purpose and recommit ourselves to Torah and *mitzvos*. So much time has already been lost, but there is always an opportunity to mend our wrongs. Our sages tell us, "The words of Torah only endure through those who slay themselves over it." (Brachos 6b)

Rabbi Akiva started his pursuit of Torah at the ripe old age of forty and had thousands of students. In Megilah 6b it says, "[if someone tells you] 'I worked hard and found [the truth],' believe him. [But if he tells you] 'I worked hard and did not find,' [or] 'I did not work hard, but I found', do not believe him.'" As it says in Bamidbar 19:14, "This is the Torah: When a man dies in the tent."

The Talmud states, "He who humbles himself for the sake of the Torah in this world is magnified in the next, and he who makes himself a servant to the [study of the] Torah in this world becomes free in the next." (Baba Metzia 85b)

The Talmud says, "Just as light protects forever, so Torah protects forever." And it says, "When you walk, it will guide you; when you lie down, it will watch over you; when you wake up, it will advocate for you." (Sota 21a) Therefore, the Torah "is not in Heaven." *Hashem* could have given the Torah to the angels or the luminaries. But He didn't; He gave it to you. Now it is up to you to realize the great gift you have been given and to use it as your guidebook to live a holy life. A life higher than the angels. One unreachable by anyone else but a simple Jew.

Lesson 23

"יִהְיוּ לְרָצוֹן אִמְרֵי פִי וְהֶגְיוֹן לִבִּי
לְפָנֶיךָ"

*"... the meditation of my heart be acceptable
before thee." (Psalms 19:14)*

We end the *Shemona Esray* prayer with the words, "יִהְיוּ
לְרָצוֹן אִמְרֵי פִי וְהֶגְיוֹן לִבִּי לְפָנֶיךָ". It is the same *gematria Mispar
Katan* reduced as the word האמין (106), which means to believe.
When we believe in our own prayer and *Hashem's* ability to
answer, then (106) אעלה; it goes up and ascends through the
gates. (106) א-י-ה-ל-כ-ם, *Hashem* becomes your G-d, but when
we don't believe, קאה (106) then the words are vomited out,
rejected.

If you take just the words my heart is before you, לִבִּי
תלְפָנֶיךָ you have the same *gematria* in *Mispar Siduri* as the word
כלים (100) vessels. If a person places his heart completely
before *Hashem*, even if it's only in simple faith, that is enough
to make him a vessel for G-d's light and salvation. Then, יגאלנו
(100); then He will redeem him and fix all his problems. It also
invokes the power of the holy name נלך (100), which is one of
the 72 Holy names of *Hashem*, which also means 'to go'. The
person will go out from his problems and dwell in the light of
Hashem.

How do you put your heart before *Hashem*? Through
teshuva, repentance. Wherever you are in your life, you can also
purify your heart that moment as all *Hashem* desires is a pure
heart before Him. "Create in me a clean heart, oh G-d; and
renew a right spirit within me." (Psalm 51:10)

Lesson 24

"כָּל הַמְחֻבָּר לַטָּמֵא, טָמֵא. וְהַמְחֻבָּר
לַטָהוֹר, טָהוֹר"

"All that is connected to something Tamei (impure) is Tamei and all that is connected to something Tahor (pure) is Tahor." (Keilim 12:2)

Abram said to Lot... "Separate Thyself, I pray thee, from me; as if to say, thou art not worthy to associate with me. Abram separated from him and refused to accompany or join him, since whoever associates with a sinner eventually follows in his footsteps and so brings punishment upon himself." (Zohar I, 84a)

It may not even be that the person sinful, even being around someone like Lot who had also had negative thoughts about avodas Hashem, could be enough that Abram would want to push him away. We have to learn from this how important it is to make a גדר *geder*, fence around ourselves to avoid negative influences from seeping in. גדר is the same *gematria* (207) as the word אור ohr, light. When a person creates a fence between himself and negative influences, he increases the light of the *Shechinah* in his life. We see this from the words, אין סוף, *ein sof*, which is similarly the gematria 207. The *Ein Sof* is the highest light one can connect to and this holy light is infinite.

Thinking negative all the time is like a contagious disease; you affect everyone around you with bad energy. If you stuck in a rut, try to pretend to be positive until its second nature to you. Limit your contact with people who pull you down... Don't fool yourself into hanging around with negative thinking people and people who are stuck in a materialistic lifestyle. In the end, you will only suffer from such relationships. Begin by talking on the phone less, spend more time with you and *Hashem*. Stay positive and uplifted at all times!

"כל המתובר לטמא טמא כל המחובר לטהור טהור"

"Whomever is around pure things, becomes pure, whoever is around negative things becomes impure." Also mentioned in Baba Kama 92b, If you take just the words "כל המתובר לטמא טמא" (whatever is around impurity becomes impure) in *gematria mispar sidurei* it equals 59, you have the same word as *niddah* which is 59. Therefore, in order escape impurity, you have to STAY AWAY FROM IT. You know what else is 59, גוים (other nations). If you want to have a positive, happy and successful life with Hashem, you have to spend your time with other Jews who know about Hashem and not follow the way goyim dress, act, talk or how they spend their time. If you watch videos & shows of goyim, how will you act different and separate from their ways? Step by step, you have to pull yourself away into a life surrounded only by holiness!

The *gematria* of טמא is 50, as there are 50 levels of impurity a person can fall too. However, when *Hashem* created the world, He always made opposites on both sides in order to allow for free choice. There is also the concept of the 50 Gates of the *Sefirah* of understanding.

The first source is from the Bible, from the end of the book of Job. The 50 questions G-d asks of Job correspond to the 50 Gates of Understanding.

The second source is from the Zohar, which derives the 50 Gates of Understanding from 50 times that the Exodus from Egypt is mentioned in the Five Books of Moses.

If you take the word, טהור (pure), its *gematria mispar Siduri* equals 40. This is because it takes just 40 days to change any evil trait into good and thereby become purified. In the story of Noah, the rain poured for 40 days, and submerged the world in water. Moses was on Mt. Sinai for 40 days and came down with the stone tablets. The Jews arrived at Mt. Sinai as a nation of Egyptian slaves, but after 40 days they were transformed into G-d's nation.

According to the Talmud, it takes 40 days for an embryo to be formed in its mother's womb. If one were to go cold turkey on any trait of *tuma* for 40 says, they will sorely find the strength to overcome it.

If you take just the words, "כל המחובר לטהור טהור" (all that is connected to something *tahor* (pure) is *tahor*), you get the *gematria Mispar Katan* 79. That is the same as the word, עזב *AwZov* (help). The Talmud (Shabbos 104a) informs us that someone who comes to purify himself is assisted from On High.

The *Midrash Ne'elam* explains this statement according to Rebbe Nathan who said, "The souls of the righteous come and help him."

This is the type of heavenly assistance that may be granted. The soul of a *tzaddik* will descend and become impregnated within the soul of a person who sets out to purify himself.

In layman's terms, when you do a mitzvah and seek to be holy, sparks from above can become attached to you. We always speak about the importance of lifting up sparks when we do good deeds and *mitzvos* but not enough about the daas we receive from above in return. The reason to perform *mitzvos* is not just to elevate below to above but also to draw down light through all the *Sefiros*. However, if we think we can come to higher levels of purity without prayer, we are mistaken. That is unless our Torah study is on such a lofty level. Therefore, we must constantly pray to Hashem for assistance in turning ourselves into a pure vessel for His light. King David constantly seeks out G-d, asking that he purify him.

"לֵב טָהוֹר בְּרָא־לִי אֱלֹהִים וְרוּחַ נָכוֹן חַדֵּשׁ בְּקִרְבִּי"

"Create in me a pure heart, O G-d, and renew a steadfast spirit within me." (Psalms 51:10) If you take just the first letter of every word לטב לאו נחב, you receive the same *gematria* (138) as the original *posuk*,

"כָּל הַמְחֻבָּר לַטָּמֵא, טָמֵא וְהַמְחֻבָּר לַטָּהוֹר, טָהוֹר" which totals 138 in *gematria mispar katan*. The combination לטב לאו נחב is a known Kabbalistic meditation (Sharshay Shamos p. 372) for purity and is very much connected to this idea of free choice which is given to us all, to choose between holiness and impurity. This also goes to emphasis how important it is to place a fence before your friends and surroundings, only allowing what is pure to get close to you. Don't make excuses for tuma, saying, "It won't affect me." Rather do what is necessary for your survival and have no other dealings with negativity. I equate negativity to *tuma* because that really defines it in most cases. Each Jew has an extra sensitive soul that feels good and bad more profoundly. You know what else is 138? The word חמץ (leaven). All year long, in its proper time, חמץ is fine to eat; however, during *Pesach*, it is harmful. You can't just suddenly become religious and know how to fully keep the *halachos* of *Pesach*. Studying Torah is essential. Learn the fine details of what is חמץ and what is not. The same thing is true in the case of purity. A person can't differentiate what is pure or impure in their life if they don't immerse themselves inside the Torah. Even after they are knowledgeable, they still must perceiver all the more into the deeper depths of the Torah to reach that next level of purity and closeness to Hashem. The greatest of Talmudist would say a prayer before their study of the Talmud saying, "May I not say regarding something which is *tamei* that it is *tahor*, and not regarding something which is *tahor* that is *tamei*." If scholars are so great, why would they need to worry so much about making mistakes? Because, we are taught, "Do not trust yourself until the day you die." (Berachos 29a)

Pinchas ben Yair said, "Torah leads to carefulness; carefulness leads to alacrity; alacrity leads to cleanliness; cleanliness leads to separation; separation leads to purity; purity leads to saintliness; saintliness leads to humbleness; humbleness leads to fear of sin; fear of sin leads to holiness; holiness leads to Divine Spirit." (Avodah Zarah 20b)

Reb Moshe Steinerman

Glossary

Amalek- Nation of Amalek
Aron- Ark
Bais Hamikdosh- Holy Temple
Bar – Son
Ben Torah- Someone who accepts to perform the commandments in the Torah
Binah- Understanding
Blats- Pages of Talmud
Bris- Covenant with Hashem
Bris milah- The performance of the mitzvah of circumcision
Chatzos- Midday or Midnight
Chazal- Sages
Chesed- Kindness
Chochmah- Wisdom
Daas- Understanding
Dovid HaMelech- King David
D'vekus- Closeness to G-d
Eitz hadas- Forbidden fruit
Emunah- Faith
Eretz Hakodesh- Holy Land (of Israel)
Gan Eden- Garden of Eden
Gaon- Great Rabbinical Scholar
Gehenna- Purgatory, the spiritual realm in which the souls are cleansed from blemishes brought about by their conduct on Earth
Gevurah- Might
Hanhagos- Stringencies in Jewish Customs or laws
Har Sinai- The mountain where Moses received the Torah
Hashem- G-d
Hod- Majesty
Kadosh- Holy
Kapores- Ritual of using chickens to cast one's sins upon before Yom Kippur
Karbonos- Ritual sacrifices
Kedusha- Holiness
Keruvim- Referring to the monument in the Temple
Kesser- Crown
Kohen Gadol- High Priest that served in the Temple
Limud Torah- The study of Torah
Malachim- Angels
Malchus- Kingship
Manna- Heavenly food given from above during the exodus from Egypt
Mazel- Destiny
Megillah- Scroll of Esther read on the Holiday of Purim
Melacha- Work

Menorah- Candelabra used in the Temple & during Chanukah

Mesugal- A bit crazy

Mezuzos- A scroll placed on doorposts of Jewish homes, containing a section from the Torah and often enclosed in a decorative case.

Midos- Character Traits

Midrash / Midrashic- Collections of various Rabbinic commentaries on the Tanach

Mikvah- Ritual Bath house

Mishna- The first compilation of the oral law, authored by Rabbi Yehudah HaNasi; the germinal statements of law elucidated by the Gemara

Mitzvah / Mitzvos- Commandment(s)

Moshe Rabbeinu- Moses, Greatest prophet who ever lived.

Moshiach- *The anointed one*, who will herald in a new era for Judaism and all humankind.

Mussar- The study of character correction

Netzach- Conquest

Ohel Mo'ed- Tent of Meeting

Parashah- Weekly portion of the Torah read on Shabbos

Parnasa- Income

Perek Shira- Passages of the songs of animals

Posuk- Verse, Verses

Purim- Holiday of Purim

Remez- Meaning "hint" in reference to scriptural interpretations

Sefiros- The sefiros represent the various stages of the Divine creative process, whereby G-d generated the progression of created realms culminating in our finite physical universe. The sefiros constitute the interacting components of a single metaphysical structure whose imprint can be identified at all levels and within all aspects of Creation

Selah- So shall be

Shechinah- The Divine Presence

Shefa- Blessing from Heaven

Shema- A prayer that serves as a centerpiece of the morning and evening prayers

Shlomo HaMelech- King Solomon

Simcha- Joy and celebrations

Sinai- Short for Har Sinai, the mountain in which we received the Torah

Tanach- Acronym of Torah (Law), Nevi'im (Prophets) and Ketuvim (Writings). Written Torah

Teshuva- Repentance

Tiferes- Beauty

Tikkun- Repairing

Tikkun Chatzos- (lit. "Midnight service"); a prayer recited by pious Jews at midnight, lamenting the destruction of the Holy Temple

Tzaddikim- Lit. Righteous person(s). A completely righteous person often believed to have special, mystical power.

Urim ve'tumim- Among the garments of the High Priest used for obtaining oracles.

Yeshivos- High Schools for Torah learning for boys

Yesod- Foundation

Yovel- The Jubilee year, the fiftieth year of the Shemittah cycle, during which all properties return to their original owners and all slaves are freed

Zeir Anpin- - (Aramaic., lit. "the small face"); the term used by the Kabbalah for the Divine attributes which parallel emotions

Zion- Land of Israel

Made in the USA
Columbia, SC
14 September 2018